German Essentials FOR DUMMIES®

by Wendy Foster,
Pauline Christensen, PhD,
and Anne Fox

WILEY

John Wiley & Sons, Inc.

German Essentials For Dummies®
Published by
John Wiley & Sons, Inc.
111 River St.
Hoboken, NJ 07030-5774
www.wiley.com

For general information on our other products and services, please contact our Customer Care Department within the U.S. at 877-762-2974, outside the U.S. at 317-572-3993, or fax 317-572-4002.

For technical support, please visit www.wiley.com/techsupport.

Wiley publishes in a variety of print and electronic formats and by print-on-demand. Some material included with standard print versions of this book may not be included in e-books or in print-on-demand. If this book refers to media such as a CD or DVD that is not included in the version you purchased, you may download this material at http://booksupport.wiley.com. For more information about Wiley products, visit www.wiley.com.

Library of Congress Control Number: 2012936850

ISBN 978-1-118-18422-6 (pbk); ISBN 978-1-118-22751-0 (ebk); ISBN 978-1-118-24038-0 (ebk); ISBN 978-1-118-26510-9 (ebk)

Manufactured in the United States of America

10 9 8 7 6

WILEY

About the Authors

Wendy Foster has been working as a teacher, writer, editor, and translator for longer than she can remember. She holds a German language diploma from the Language and Interpreting Institute, Munich, Germany, an MA in French from Middlebury College, Middlebury, Vermont, and a public school teaching certificate for German and French. She studied in France for two years before settling in Munich, Germany, where she worked in various teaching and writing capacities at several institutions, including Siemens, HypoVereinsbank, Munich Chamber of Commerce, and a number of publishers. She recently returned to her New England roots, where she works from her home overlooking a spectacular salt marsh that constantly beckons her to go kayaking, swimming, walking, and bird-watching.

Pauline Christensen has been working as a writer, editor, and translator for almost ten years. She holds a degree in English and German literature and has developed, written, and edited numerous German-language textbooks and teachers' handbooks for Berlitz International. Her work as a translator ranges from new media art to science fiction (*Starlog* magazine). She occasionally works as a court interpreter and does consulting and interpreting at educational conferences, as well as voice-overs for educational videos and CD-ROMs. Dr. Christensen received her MA and PhD from Düsseldorf University, Germany, and has taught at Berlitz Language Schools, New York University, and Fordham University.

Anne Fox has been working as a translator, editor, and writer for the past twelve years. She studied at Interpreters' School, Zurich, Switzerland, and holds a degree in translation. Her various assignments have taken her to outer space, hyperspace, and around the world. She has also taught at Berlitz Language Schools and worked as a legal and technical proofreader in the editorial departments of several law firms. Most recently she has been developing, writing, and editing student textbooks and teachers' handbooks for Berlitz.

DEC 2016

Publisher's Acknowledgments

We're proud of this book; please send us your comments at http://dummies.custhelp.com. For other comments, please contact our Customer Care Department within the U.S. at 877-762-2974, outside the U.S. at 317-572-3993, or fax 317-572-4002.

Some of the people who helped bring this book to market include the following:

Acquisitions, Editorial, and Vertical Websites

Project Editor: Jennifer Tebbe

Acquisitions Editor: Michael Lewis

Copy Editor: Jennette ElNaggar

Assistant Editor: David Lutton

Editorial Program Coordinator: Joe Niesen

Technical Editors: Candis Carey, Fran Reigle

Editorial Manager: Christine Meloy Beck

Editorial Assistants: Rachelle S. Amick, Alexa Koschier

Cover Photo: © iStockphoto.com/ Francesco Carucci

Cartoons: Rich Tennant (www.the5thwave.com)

Composition Services

Project Coordinator: Katie Crocker

Layout and Graphics: Claudia Bell, Corrie Niehaus

Proofreader: Bryan Coyle, John Greenough

Indexer: Potomac Indexing, LLC

Publishing and Editorial for Consumer Dummies

　　Kathleen Nebenhaus, Vice President and Executive Publisher

　　Kristin Ferguson-Wagstaffe, Product Development Director

　　Ensley Eikenburg, Associate Publisher, Travel

　　Kelly Regan, Editorial Director, Travel

Publishing for Technology Dummies

　　Andy Cummings, Vice President and Publisher

Composition Services

　　Debbie Stailey, Director of Composition Services

Contents at a Glance

Table of Contents

Chapter 7: Stepping Back in the Past 109

Chapter 8: Focusing on the Future 125

Chapter 9: Understanding Verb Moods 135

Introduction

$\displaystyle\gamma$ ou may be taking a German course in high school or college, or perhaps you're interested in refreshing your German because you're planning to spend some time in German-speaking Europe. Using this practical reference book to help you advance your German is a great means of making measurable progress — fast. How? Well, this book offers you straight talk as it leads you through a review of the key material you need to understand the basic level of German.

German Essentials For Dummies provides you easy access to practical information that helps you communicate successfully in German. You find the basic grammar that you encounter in introductory German courses. You see clearly what you need to know in order to express yourself in spoken and written German. This book guides you down the path to conversing with confidence in the kinds of situations you encounter on a daily basis when interacting with German speakers. So get a head start and be ready to speak, write, and travel **in Deutschland** (*in Germany*).

About This Book

German Essentials For Dummies gives you straight talk, the nitty-gritty, and just enough detail to see you successfully through any major roadblocks to communicating in German. You find a good balance between important grammar points and useful, communicative language. Without even realizing it, your German vocabulary expands as you cruise through the book.

Each chapter is self-contained, making this a very user-friendly reference. You can go through it in any order you choose, zeroing in on your priorities. This book is practical and accessible, whether you're looking for a clear overview of what you've covered in coursework or to reactivate the German you acquired a while back.

Conventions Used in This Book

I use a couple conventions in this book to help you spot essential elements in the text:

- ✔ I **boldface** German words and example sentences. I also **boldface** word endings to make them easier to recognize.

- ✔ I *italicize* English equivalents that accompany German words and sentences.

Foolish Assumptions

In writing *German Essentials For Dummies,* I made the following assumptions about who you are and what you aim to achieve from this book:

- ✔ You've acquired at least a smattering of spoken and written German in high school or at the college level.

- ✔ You want to do some review so you can pass a test or get to the next level of German by taking a placement exam.

- ✔ You want to expand your knowledge of German so you feel comfortable in both speaking and writing the language. (Alternatively, you want to dream in German.)

- ✔ You're enthusiastic about honing your German skills because you use German in school, you do business with German speakers, or you intend to do some traveling in German-speaking countries.

Icons Used in This Book

Throughout this book, I include icons in the left-hand margin to draw your attention to valuable information. Here's what each icon means.

Pay attention to these key points. By noticing how German differs from English, you see patterns that show you how to assemble German into meaningful statements.

This icon alerts you to key information that's worth remembering. Stash this info in your mind because you'll end up using it again and again.

Useful points that help you absorb German more easily and effectively await you when you see this icon.

Where to Go from Here

Wondering where to start? Try scanning the Table of Contents and selecting a chapter that piques your interest. Or use the index to look up a specific point you're interested in reading about. Basically, you don't need to follow the chapters in sequence because each chapter contains a discrete topic, so you can dig in to the information in any order you choose. Of course, there's nothing stopping you from going ahead in a linear fashion if that's your style. Just make sure you're enjoying the process of soaking up the core concepts of German.

Chapter 1 takes you through some fundamentals of German, so you may want to check it out first to make sure you're familiar with the topics and basic vocabulary covered there. Other than that, feel free to go at your own pace, proceeding in any order you choose. Skip over sections you're not ready to do yet or don't need to read right away. Most important, wherever you go in this book, **Viel Spaß!** (*Have a lot of fun!*)

The 5th Wave

By Rich Tennant

©RICHTENNANT

SPEAKING GERMAN

"Let's see, 'telephone number' is 'telefonnummer,' 'accelerator' is 'gaspedal,' 'telephone book' is 'telefonbuch'... I get the feeling German is just English without the space bar."

Chapter 1

Laying the Foundations of German

In This Chapter

▶ Counting with cardinal and ordinal numbers

▶ Stating dates and times

▶ Pointing out the parts of speech

*F*amiliarizing yourself with how to use numbers, time, and dates is basic to your German skills. Understanding parts of speech will get you ahead in using spoken and written German.

Crunching the Numbers

You encounter the two types of numbers, cardinals and ordinals, in myriads of situations. *Cardinal numbers* are vital for counting, prices, phone numbers, or for communicating time and dates. You use *ordinal numbers,* such as first, second, and third, to express a floor number or which street you take when following directions (like when someone tells you to take the third street on your left). The following sections go into detail about using both types of numbers.

1-2-3: Counting off with cardinal numbers

Table 1-1 shows numbers 1 through 29. Notice a couple of points about numbers 21 and up:

✔ They're written as one word: **einundzwanzig** (*21*), **zwei-undzwanzig** (*22*).

✔ They follow the cart-before-the-horse rule — that is, you say the ones digit before the tens digit, linking the words with **und:** for example, **vierundzwanzig** (*24;* literally: *four and twenty*).

Table 1-1   Cardinal Numbers 1–29

Numbers 0–9	Numbers 10–19	Numbers 20–29
0 null	10 zehn	20 zwanzig
1 eins	11 elf	21 einundzwanzig
2 zwei	12 zwölf	22 zweiundzwanzig
3 drei	13 dreizehn	23 dreiundzwanzig
4 vier	14 vierzehn	24 vierundzwanzig
5 fünf	15 fünfzehn	25 fünfundzwanzig
6 sechs	16 sechzehn	26 sechsundzwanzig
7 sieben	17 siebzehn	27 siebenundzwanzig
8 acht	18 achtzehn	28 achtundzwanzig
9 neun	19 neunzehn	29 neunundzwanzig

In spoken German, people commonly use **zwo** instead of **zwei,** which avoids the confusion — acoustically speaking — with **drei.** To double-check that you heard **zwei** and not **drei** in credit card numbers, prices, telephone numbers, room numbers, and so on, either ask or repeat the number(s), using **zwo.** Say, for example, **Ich wiederhole vier-zwo-acht** (*I'll repeat four-two-eight*). If you're still not sure of the numbers even after repeating them back to the speaker, try the failsafe route — ask for them via e-mail: **E-mailen Sie mir bitte diese Zahlen/ihre Telefonnummer.** (*Please e-mail me these numbers/your telephone number.*) In writing, the number two is always **zwei.**

Table 1-2 shows representative numbers spanning 30 to 999. Double-digit numbers follow the same pattern as 21 to 29 do in Table 1-1: **einunddreißig** (*31;* literally: *one and thirty*), **zweiunddreißig** (*32;* literally: *two and thirty*), and the like. Numbers with more digits likewise flip the ones and tens digits: For example, you'd read *384* as **dreihundertvierundachtzig,** which literally means *three hundred four and eighty.*

Note that 30, unlike the other multiples of ten (40, 50, and so on) is spelled slightly differently. **Dreißig** has no **z** in its ending, whereas the other double-digits do (**vierzig, fünfzig,** and so on).

Table 1-2   **Cardinal Numbers 30–999**

Numbers 30–100	*Numbers 101–114*	*Numbers 220–999*
30 **dreißig**	101 **hunderteins**	220 **zweihundertzwanzig**
40 **vierzig**	102 **hundertzwei**	348 **dreihundertachtundvierzig**
50 **fünfzig**	103 **hundertdrei**	452 **vierhundertzweiundfünfzig**
60 **sechzig**	104 **hundertvier**	573 **fünfhundertdreiundsiebzig**
70 **siebzig**	111 **hundertelf**	641 **sechshunderteinundvierzig**
80 **achtzig**	112 **hundertzwölf**	767 **siebenhundertsiebenundsechzig**
90 **neunzig**	113 **hundertdreizehn**	850 **achthundertfünfzig**
100 **hundert**	114 **hundertvierzehn**	999 **neunhundertneunundneunzig**

In German, people often say telephone numbers in double digits, so you need to be super careful to get the sequence correct as you write the number. For example, the number 76 20 93 88 would be **sechsundsiebzig, zwanzig, dreiundneunzig, achtundachtzig** (*six and seventy, twenty, three and ninety, eight and eighty*).

Especially in spoken German, you can use **einhundert** (*one hundred*) instead of **hundert** (*hundred*). Doing so makes the number clearer to the listener.

When referring to currency, you can talk about the bills like this: Imagine you're cashing 400€ in traveler's checks and you want three 100€ bills and five 20€ bills. You say: **Ich möchte drei Hunderter und fünf Zwanziger.** (*I'd like three hundreds [euro bills] and five twenties.*) The numbers **Hunderter** and **Zwanziger** are nouns, and you form them like this: Take the number, for example **hundert,** and add **-er** to the end of the number: **hundert + -er = Hunderter.**

For numbers higher than 999, look at Table 1-3. Notice that the decimal point in German numbers represents the comma in English.

Table 1-3		Numbers Greater Than 999
English Numerals	*German Numerals*	*Numbers Written in German*
1,000	1.000	tausend or ein tausend
1,000,000	1.000.000	Million or eine Milllion
1,650,000	1.650.000	eine Million sechshundertfünzigtausend
2,000,000	2.000.000	zwei Millionen
1,000,000,000	1.000.000.000	eine Milliarde
2,000,000,000	2.000.000.000	zwei Milliarden

In English, a comma indicates thousands and a period shows decimals. German (and many other languages) does the reverse: It uses a period (**Punkt**) for thousands and the comma (**Komma**) as a decimal point. Look at these examples:

English: 1 inch = 2.54 centimeters

Deutsch: 1 **Zentimeter** (*centimeters*) = **0,39 Zoll** (*inches*) 0,39 is read as **null Komma drei neun.**

English: Mount Everest is 29,029 feet high.

Deutsch: **Mount Everest ist 8.848 Meter hoch.** 8.848 is read as **achttausendachthundertachtundvierzig.**

1st, 2nd, 3rd: Lining up with ordinal numbers

Ordinal numbers are the kinds of numbers that show what order things come in. You need ordinal numbers when you're talking about **das Datum** (*the date*), **die Feiertage** (*the holidays*), **die Stockwerke in einem Hotel** (*the floors in a hotel*), and stuff like that.

Ordinal numbers function as adjectives, so they have the adjective endings you normally use in a sentence. (See Chapter 5 for specifics on adjectives.) The general rule for forming ordinal numbers is to add **-te** to the numbers 1 through 19 and then **-ste** to the numbers 20 and above. For example: **Nach der achten Tasse Kaffee, ist er am Schreibtisch eingeschlafen.** (*After the eighth cup of coffee, he fell asleep on the desk.*)

The three exceptions to this rule are **erste** (*first*), **dritte** (*third*), and **siebte** (*seventh*). For example: **Reinhold Messner war der erste Mensch, der Mount Everest ohne Sauerstoffmaske bestieg.** (*Reinhold Messner was the first person to climb Mt. Everest without an oxygen mask.*)

Two other adjectives you need to know when putting things in order are **letzte** (*last*) and **nächste** (*next*). You can use them to refer to a sequence of numbers, people, things, or the like:

> **Könnten Sie bitte die letzte Nummer wiederholen?**
> (*Could you repeat the last number, please?*)

Look at the examples of ordinal numbers in Table 1-4. The first column shows the ordinal numbers as digits, the second column shows the same ordinal numbers as words, and the third column shows how to say *on the (fifth floor, 12th day of Christmas, and so on).*

Note: In Table 1-4, you see how to formulate the expression *on the (first).* It's **am** + *ordinal number* + **en. Am** is the contraction of **an** (*on*) + **dem** (*the*) and is formed by taking the preposition **an** plus **dem,** the masculine dative of **der.** You need to show dative case agreement with the adjective **erste,** so you add **-n: erste** + **n** = **ersten.**

Table 1-4	Ordinal Numbers	
Ordinals as Numerals	*Ordinals as Words*	*On the . . .*
1st	**der erste** (*the first*)	**am ersten** (*on the first*)
2nd	**der zweite** (*the second*)	**am zweiten** (*on the second*)
3rd	**der dritte** (*the third*)	**am dritten** (*on the third*)
4th	**der vierte** (*the fourth*)	**am vierten** (*on the fourth*)
5th	**der fünfte** (*the fifth*)	**am fünften** (*on the fifth*)

(continued)

Table 1-4 (continued)

Ordinals as Numerals	Ordinals as Words	On the . . .
6th	der sechste (the sixth)	am sechsten (on the sixth)
7th	der siebte (the seventh)	am siebten (on the seventh)
18th	der achtzehnte (the eighteenth)	am achtzehnten (on the eighteenth)
22nd	der zweiundzwanzigste (the twenty-second)	am zweiundzwanzigsten (on the twenty-second)

Expressing Dates

Familiarizing yourself with the German calendar words, as discussed in the following sections, makes scheduling a meeting or planning a trip much simpler.

Looking at the week

On a German calendar, *the week* (**die Woche**) starts on Monday. In addition, the days of the week are all the same gender, masculine (**der**), but generally they're used without an article. For example, if you want to say that today is *Monday,* you say, **Heute ist Montag.**

Here are the days of the week followed by the abbreviations you often see on schedules:

- ✔ **Montag** (Mo) (*Monday*)
- ✔ **Dienstag** (Di) (*Tuesday*)
- ✔ **Mittwoch** (Mi) (*Wednesday*)
- ✔ **Donnerstag** (Do) (*Thursday*)
- ✔ **Freitag** (Fr) (*Friday*)
- ✔ **Samstag/Sonnabend** (Sa) (*Saturday*)
- ✔ **Sonntag** (So) (*Sunday*)

Note: In northern Germany, *Saturday* is called **Sonnabend;** people living in southern Germany, Austria, and German-speaking Switzerland use the term **Samstag.**

To indicate that something always happens on a particular day of the week, an **s** is added to the word, and it's no longer capitalized. For example, you may get to a museum or a restaurant on a Monday and find it closed, in which case you're likely to see a sign on the door reading **montags geschlossen** (*closed on Mondays*).

Speaking of days: Pretend it's Tuesday, and you want to confirm your plans to meet someone the next day. You can ask whether you're meeting on Wednesday or whether the meeting is tomorrow. The following word list helps you refer to specific days:

- **heute** (*today*)
- **gestern** (*yesterday*)
- **vorgestern** (*the day before yesterday*)
- **morgen** (*tomorrow*)
- **übermorgen** (*the day after tomorrow*)

To speak precisely about a particular time on a specific day, you can combine the preceding words with the times of day discussed in the later section "Talking about parts of the day." Try on the following examples for size:

heute Morgen (*this morning*)

heute Vormittag (*this morning*)

gestern Abend (*yesterday evening/last night*)

Naming the months

The following list shows you all the names of the months — notice how similar the German names are to the English. All the months' names are masculine, meaning their article is **der:**

- **Januar** (*January*)
- **Februar** (*February*)

✔ **März** (*March*)

✔ **April** (*April*)

✔ **Mai** (*May*)

✔ **Juni** (*June*)

✔ **Juli** (*July*)

✔ **August** (*August*)

✔ **September** (*September*)

✔ **Oktober** (*October*)

✔ **November** (*November*)

✔ **Dezember** (*December*)

The following sentences show you how to build the *calendar* (**der Kalender**) in German:

> **Ein Jahr hat 12 Monate.** (*A year has 12 months.*)
>
> **Ein Monat hat 30 oder 31 Tage.** (*A month has 30 or 31 days.*)
>
> **Der Februar hat 28 oder 29 Tage.** (*February has 28 or 29 days.*)
>
> **Eine Woche hat 7 Tage.** (*A week has seven days.*)

 In order to write dates as numerals, write the digit followed by a period: **Der 1. Mai ist ein Feiertag in Deutschland.** (*May 1st is a holiday in Germany.*) If you say the same sentence, it's **Der erste Mai ist ein Feiertag in Deutschland.**

Telling Time

Imagine you're sitting in a park under a tree on a hot sunny day, wondering what time it is. Suddenly, a white rabbit in a checkered jacket runs by, stops, pulls out a pocket watch, and mumbles about being late. Here are two ways you can ask him or anyone else what time it is:

> **Wie viel Uhr ist es?** (*What time is it?*)
>
> **Wie spät ist es?** (*What time is it?*)

German speakers have two systems for telling time: One uses the numbers 1 through 12 on a standard clock, and one uses a 24-hour format. They use the 12-hour system in casual conversation and the 24-hour system when they want to avoid any chance of misunderstanding. *Note:* German speakers don't use the a.m./p.m. system.

Using the 12-hour clock

At the top of any hour, telling the time is very easy. You just say **Es ist . . . Uhr.** (*It's . . . o'clock.*)

Of course, you include the number of the appropriate hour before the word **Uhr: Es ist acht Uhr.** (*It's eight o'clock.*)

Indicating times such as quarter past three, ten to eight, or half past eleven is a little more complicated, but you need to know only three key expressions. To use the German word for quarter, you include **Viertel** (*quarter*) plus the word **nach** (*past/after*) or **vor** (*to/before*) followed by the appropriate hour, as shown in these examples:

> **Es ist Viertel nach . . .** (*It's quarter past . . .*)
>
> **Es ist Viertel vor . . .** (*It's quarter to . . .*)

Expressing the half hour isn't quite as straightforward. In German, the word **halb** (*half*) indicates half of the hour to come, rather than the past hour. You use the phrase **Es ist halb . . .** (*It's half an hour before . . .*) followed by the appropriate hour. For example, when it's 4:30, you say this:

> **Es ist halb fünf.** (*It's half an hour before 5:00./It's four thirty./It's half past four.*)
>
> **Es ist halb sieben.** (*It's half an hour before 7:00./It's six thirty./It's half past six.*)

When you need to break down the time in terms of minutes before or after the hour, you use **nach** (*past/after*) and **vor** (*to/before*), like this:

> **Es ist fünf vor zwölf.** (*It's five [minutes] to twelve.*)
>
> **Es ist zwanzig nach sechs.** (*It's twenty [minutes] past six.*)

Using the 24-hour system

All kinds of businesses — from banks, stores, and airlines to theaters, museums, and cinemas — use the 24-hour system of telling time. Here's how it works: After you reach 12, you keep adding hours (13, 14, 15, and so on) until you get to 24 or **Mitternacht** (*midnight*), which is also referred to as **null Uhr.**

In this system of telling time, you don't use phrases such as *half past* or *a quarter to* (the hour). Everything is expressed in terms of minutes after the hour. Note in the following examples how the hour comes first and then the minutes:

> **Es ist 15 Uhr dreißig.** (*It's fifteen hours and thirty.*) This corresponds to 3:30 p.m.

> **Es ist 21 Uhr fünfzehn.** (*It's twenty-one hours and fifteen.*) That's 9:15 p.m.

> **Es ist 22 Uhr vierundvierzig.** (*It's twenty-two hours and forty-four.*) You got it — 10:44 p.m.

> **Es ist null Uhr siebenundreißig.** (*It's zero hours and thirty-seven.*) That's early in the morning — 12:37 a.m!

Talking about parts of the day

When you want to describe a slice of the day, such as morning or afternoon, you have several options in German. However, take the following time periods with a grain of salt; they're meant as guidelines. After all, night owls and early morning joggers have different ideas about when one part of the day starts and another ends.

- **der Morgen** (*morning;* 4:00 a.m. to noon)
- **der Vormittag** (*morning;* 9:00 a.m. to noon)
- **der Mittag** (*noon;* 12 noon to 2:00 p.m.)
- **der Nachmitag** (*afternoon;* 2:00 p.m. to 6:00 p.m.)
- **der Abend** (*evening;* 6:00 p.m. to 12:00 a.m.)
- **die Nacht** (*tonight;* 12:00 a.m. to 4:00 a.m.)

Identifying Parts of Speech

To construct a simple sentence, you need a certain number of building blocks: the parts of speech. The most essential of these are nouns, articles, pronouns, adjectives, verbs, adverbs, and prepositions. The following sections give you the lowdown on each part of speech.

Naming with nouns and articles

A rose is a rose is a rose, right? Well, a rose is also a noun, and nouns aren't exactly the same in German and English. Although nouns in both languages name things (people, places, objects, concepts, and so on), the difference is that all German nouns are capitalized and have one of three genders: masculine, feminine, or neuter. Unfortunately, the meaning of a noun isn't usually much help in predicting that noun's grammatical gender.

In German, grammatical gender is an element of German grammar and isn't related to the meaning of the noun. Instead, it's a kind of marker that identifies how the noun fits into a sentence. Sorry, no easy way out. You simply have to memorize the gender that belongs with each noun. (Flip to Chapter 2 for help getting a grip on word gender.)

Nouns often appear in the company of a sidekick: a definite article or an indefinite article.

> ✒ **Definite articles:** Although the definite article *the* has only one form in English, it has three forms in German: **der** (masculine), **die** (feminine), and **das** (neuter). Which form you use depends on the gender of the German noun. **Der** is the definite article used with masculine nouns, **die** is used with feminine nouns, and **das** is used with neuter nouns.

When meeting a new noun, find out whether its definite article is **der, die,** or **das** — in other words, determine the gender of the noun. For example, memorize **der Garten** (*the garden*) rather than just **Garten** (*garden*), **die Tür** (*the door*) rather than **Tür** (*door*), and **das Haus** (*the house*) rather than **Haus** (*house*).

✔ **Indefinite articles:** In English, you use the indefinite article *a* or *an* when you want to specify one of a particular thing. Because you're dealing with three different genders in German, you also have to use three different indefinite articles. Luckily, the indefinite article for masculine and neuter nouns is the same, **ein.** For example, **ein Name** (*a name*) or **ein Bier** (*a beer*). For feminine nouns, you add an **e** to **ein** to make **eine.** For example, **eine Nacht** (*a night*).

Note: The endings of the articles change depending on the case of the noun they're attached to. For the scoop on case, head to Chapter 2.

Replacing with pronouns

Pronouns are the handy group of words that can punt for nouns so you don't sound redundant. In German, pronouns change form depending on their role in a sentence. For example, **ich** (*I*) can change into **mich** (*me*) or **mir** (*me*). In the following list, you find the types of pronouns you encounter in this book (see Chapter 2 for more details on each pronoun type):

✔ **Personal pronouns:** These pronouns translate to *I, you, he, she, it, we,* and *they.* You use them frequently in everyday German language.

> **Spielst du gern Karten?** (*Do you like to play cards?*)

> **Ja, ich spiele gern Poker.** (*Yes, I like to play poker.*)

✔ **Relative pronouns:** You use relative pronouns when you want to tack on some more information about a noun or a pronoun that has already been mentioned. This group includes the German equivalents of *who, whom, whose, that,* and *which.*

> **Ich kenne den Supermarkt, den du meinst.** (*I know the supermarket [that] you mean/are talking about.*)

> **Wie gefällt dir das Hemd, das ich anhabe?** (*How do you like the shirt [that] I'm wearing?*)

✔ **Demonstrative pronouns:** You make use of the demonstrative pronouns *this, that, these,* or *those* when you need to add emphasis to something or someone you're pointing out. Frequently, the demonstrative pronouns are translated as *he, him, she, her, it, they,* or *them.*

Ist <u>diese</u> Straße relativ ruhig? Ja, <u>die</u> ist absolut ruhig. (*Is <u>this</u> street relatively quiet? Yes, <u>it</u>'s absolutely quiet.*)

Wie findest du <u>diesen</u> Wein? <u>Den</u> finde ich ausgezeichnet. (*How do you like <u>this</u> wine? <u>It</u>'s outstanding.*)

What you think of in English as possessive pronouns, for example, **mein** (*my*), **dein** (*your:* singular, informal), **sein** (*his*), or **euer** (*your:* plural, informal), are considered adjectives in German because the endings they form resemble those of descriptive adjectives. Head to Chapter 5 for more on this topic.

Describing with adjectives

Adjectives describe nouns. In German, adjectives have different endings depending on the gender, case (more about that in Chapter 2), and number (singular or plural) of the noun they accompany. Adjective endings also depend on whether the adjective is accompanied by a definite article, an indefinite article, or no article at all. I help you figure out how to form adjectives properly in Chapter 5.

Conveying action with verbs

Verbs express actions or states of being. The person doing the action is the verb's subject, and the verb always adjusts its ending to the subject. For example, you say *I open the door* and *the cat opens the door.* In the present tense in English, most verbs have two different forms, or spellings: for example, *open* and *opens.* Most German verbs, on the other hand, have four different forms. (For further information on tenses, check out Chapters 3, 7, and 8.)

The verb form in its basic, static state is called the *infinitive.* It's what you see in any dictionary. In English, the infinitive verb form looks like *to ride,* and you can put it into a sentence like this: *I know how to ride a camel.* German infinitives, however, usually have the ending **-en,** as in **lachen** (*to laugh*), stuck onto what's called the *stem.* For example, the stem of **lachen** is **lach-.** A small number of verbs have the infinitive ending **-n.**

The stems of most verbs don't change, and the endings of such verbs are always the same. But some exceptions to the rule do exist. When the stem of the verb ends in **-m, -n, -d,** or **-t,** you need to insert an **-e** before the ending in the **du, er/sie/ es,** and **ihr** constructions, as in **er arbeit-e-t** (*he works*).

Modifying with adverbs

Adverbs accompany verbs or adjectives, and their purpose is to describe them. In English, most adverbs end with *-ly* (as in: I ran down the stairs *quickly.*) In German, adverbs are generally spelled the same as their adjective counterparts in their barebones form, without special endings.

For example, take **vorsichtig** (*careful/carefully*), which has the same spelling for both its adjective and its adverb meaning. When you use **vorsichtig** in a sentence as an adverb, it keeps the same spelling: **Fahren Sie vorsichtig!** (*Drive carefully!*) However, when you use **vorsichtig** in a sentence as an adjective, it changes its form (spelling) the way all German adjectives do: **Sie ist eine vorsichtige Fahrerin.** (*She's a careful driver.*)

Connecting with prepositions

A *preposition* is a small word that shows the relationship between its object (a noun) and another word or words in the sentence. It's part of a *prepositional phrase,* which starts with a preposition and has an article, noun, and other words.

You find out how crucially important these little guys are in expressing such things as the following:

- ✔ Place/where something is located, as with **in** (*in*): **Es gibt eine Fliege in meiner Suppe.** (*There's a fly in my soup.*)

- ✔ Movement/the direction where something is going, as with **unter** (*under*): **Eine Maus läuft unter meinen Stuhl.** (*A mouse is running under my chair.*)

✔ Information showing relationships, as with **trotz** (*in spite of*): **Trotz dieser Überraschungen, schmeckt mir das Essen.** (*In spite of these surprises, the food tastes good.*)

Prepositions, such as *around, before,* and *with,* combine with other words to form prepositional phrases that provide information on where (*around the corner*), when (*before noon*), who (*with you*), and much more. Prepositions perform incredible tasks when they combine with other words, notably nouns and verbs, to create a diverse range of expressions. But all those possibilities come at a price. Prepositions are finicky little critters, much more so in German than in English. They abide by grammar rules. To get more comfortable with understanding and using German prepositions, look at Chapter 5.

Building Sentences

Nouns, pronouns, verbs, adjectives, and adverbs aren't just thrown together helter-skelter; instead, to create a logical sentence, you arrange words in a specific order. The correct order is determined by certain rules, which the next sections explain.

Getting words in the right order

Standard word order in German is much like English word order. The subject comes first, then the verb, followed by the rest of the sentence. Look at the following example sentence.

Subject	Verb	Direct Object
Meine Freundin	**hat**	**einen Hund.**
My girlfriend	*has*	*a dog.*

Putting the verb in second place

One of the most important things to remember is the place of the verb in a German sentence. In freestanding clauses (known as *independent clauses*), like the one in the preceding section, a one-word verb is always in second place, no matter what. The term *second place,* however, doesn't necessarily mean the second word in the sentence. Rather, it refers to the second "placeholder," which may be comprised of more than one word. For example, **meine Freundin,** the subject of the earlier sentence, consists of two words but it's the first placeholder. In the following example, the verb is **fahren** (*to drive*), and it follows the second-place rule.

> **Meine Freundin fährt nach Dänemark.** (*My girlfriend is going to Denmark.*)

How about adding some more information?

> **Meine Freundin fährt morgen mit dem Zug nach Dänemark.** (*My girlfriend is going to Denmark by train tomorrow.*)

Standard practice in German sentences is to place the reference to time first followed by the reference to manner, and after that, the reference to place, as you can see in the previous example where **morgen** (*tomorrow*) appears first, then **mit dem Zug** (*by train*), followed by **nach Dänemark** (*to Denmark*).

What happens if you start the sentence with **morgen?**

> **Morgen fährt meine Freundin mit dem Zug nach Dänemark.** (*Tomorrow my girlfriend is going to Denmark by train.*)

Morgen is in first place, and because the verb has to be in second place, the subject follows the verb. Technically, this arrangement is called *inversion of the verb*. All it means is that the verb and the subject switch places. Inversion of the verb occurs whenever anything other than the subject occupies first place in a sentence.

Having said that, what about the statement **Meine Freundin hat einen Hund** (from the preceding section)? Can you give that one a twirl and change the word order? Absolutely, as long as the verb stays in second place, like this: **Einen Hund hat meine Freundin.** But why would you want to rearrange word order? Generally, you do so to shift emphasis in the meaning. For example, you may hear something along the lines of the following conversation:

Hat deine Schwester einen Hund? (*Does your sister have a dog?*)

Nein, sie hat eine Katze. Einen Hund hat meine Freundin Heike. (No, she has a *cat*. It's my girlfriend, Heike, who has *a dog.*)

Don't German speakers get all confused playing around with word order like that? That's where the (in)famous German case system (covered in Chapter 2) comes into play. Adjectives and articles that appear alongside nouns and, in some instances, the nouns themselves, assume different endings depending on their function in a sentence. So no matter where a noun appears in a German sentence, you can figure out its role by checking the ending of the article, the noun itself, and/or the adjective.

Placing the verb at the end

Dependent clauses typically start with *subordinating conjunctions* (words that link sentences) such as **dass** (*that*), **weil** (*because*), **damit** (*so that*), **obwohl** (*although*), **bevor** (*before*), and **wenn** (*when*). These subordinating conjunctions affect word order: They always push the verb to the end.

Check out the following sentence, which combines several thoughts to form a more complex structure:

Wir gehen nicht ins Konzert, weil wir kein Geld haben. (*We're not going to the concert because we have no money.*)

The verb **gehen** (*go*) is in second place as you would expect, but the verb **haben** (*have*) in the dependent clause beginning with **weil** gets kicked to the end.

Chapter 2

Grasping Gender and Case

*M*ost words in a German sentence take their cues from the nouns (or their esteemed representatives, the pronouns). When studying German, you really don't know a new noun unless you know its characteristics, which include gender. So for each new noun you come across, you need to accept its gender as a part of the word and commit it to memory. But that's not all.

In order to use nouns and pronouns (as well as adjectives and prepositions) in a German sentence, you need to know how they fit together; this is the role of case. Case and gender are closely linked together, and I consider them pieces of a puzzle in making German sentences.

This chapter gives you the lowdown on how gender and case work hand in hand to form various endings on the members of two large families of words: the article family and the pronoun family.

Getting a Grip on Word Gender

In German grammar, *gender* is the classification of a noun or pronoun into one of three categories: masculine, feminine, or neuter. These genders are like markers that refer to the words, not their meanings.

You can tell the gender of a German noun by observing the definite article associated with it. The three gender markers, the definite articles **der** (masculine), **die** (feminine), and **das** (neuter), all mean *the*.

Compare the following three German sentences, which are the same as the three English example sentences:

> ✔ **Kannst du das Mädchen da drüben sehen? Es ist sehr groß.** (*Can you see the girl over there? She's really tall.*) *The girl* in German is **das Mädchen,** a neuter gender noun, as are all nouns ending in -**chen.** *Remember:* The gender of a noun is simply a grammatical reference.

> ✔ **Der neue Deutschlehrer ist Herr Mangold. Ich glaube, dass er aus Bremen kommt.** (*The new German teacher is Herr Mangold. I think he comes from Bremen.*) You refer, grammatically speaking, to **Herr Mangold** as **er** (*he*). In most (but not all) cases in German, male beings are **der** nouns, and female beings are **die** nouns.

> ✔ **Hast du die tolle Gitarre im Schaufenster gesehen? Sie hat zwölf Saiten.** (*Have you seen the cool guitar in the shop window? It has 12 strings.*) Strange but true: Grammatically speaking, a guitar is feminine, so you refer to it as **sie** (*she*). Most nouns ending in -**e** are feminine nouns.

Definite articles aren't always present in sentences. Sometimes you may see an indefinite article instead, or you may not see any article at all. The following sections help you figure out how to determine gender in these situations. They also fill you in on how to form plural nouns.

Using indefinite articles

Just like English has two indefinite articles — *a* and *an* — that you use with singular nouns, German also has two indefinite articles (in the nominative case): **ein** for masculine- and neuter-gender words and **eine** for feminine-gender words. (Remember that with German nouns, the gender functions purely as a grammatical marker.)

An indefinite article has many of the same uses in both languages. For example, you use it before a singular noun that's countable the first time it's mentioned — **Ein Mann geht um die Ecke** (*A man is walking around the corner*). You also use it when a singular countable noun represents a class of things; for example: **Ein Elefant vergisst nie** (*An elephant never forgets*). You can even use **ein/eine** together with a *predicate noun* (a noun that complements the subject, such as the underlined word in the following example): **Willy Brandt war ein geschickter** <u>Politiker</u> (*Willy Brandt was a skillful <u>politician</u>*).

Here's how the definite articles and the indefinite articles (nominative case) correspond.

Gender/Number	Definite (the)	Indefinite (a/an)
Masculine	**der**	**ein**
Feminine	**die**	**eine**
Neuter	**das**	**ein**
Plural	**die**	(no plural form)

Note: The German indefinite article **ein/eine** has no plural form.

Some categories of nouns are consistently masculine, feminine, or neuter. For example, noun gender usually does follow the gender of people: **der Onkel** (*the uncle*), **die Schwester** (*the sister*). Most often, the noun groups have to do with the ending of the noun. Look at Tables 2-1 and 2-2 (note, however, that exceptions do exist).

Table 2-1   Common Genders by Noun Ending (or Beginning)

Usually Masculine (der)	Usually Feminine (die)	Usually Neuter (das)
-er (especially when referring to male people/jobs)	**-ade, -age, -anz, -enz, -ette, -ine, -ion, -tur** (if foreign/borrowed from another language)	**-chen**
-ich	**-e**	**-ium**
-ismus	**-ei**	**-lein**
-ist	**-heit**	**-ment** (if foreign/borrowed from another language)

(continued)

Table 2-1 *(continued)*

Usually Masculine (der)	Usually Feminine (die)	Usually Neuter (das)
-ner	-ie	-o
	-ik	-tum or -um
	-in (when referring to female people/occupations)	Starting with Ge-
	-keit	
	-schaft	
	-tät	
	-ung	

Table 2-2 Common Noun Genders by Subject

Usually Masculine (der)	Usually Feminine (die)	Usually Neuter (das)
Days, months, and seasons: der Freitag (*Friday*)	Many flowers: die Rose (*the rose*)	Colors (adjectives) used as nouns: grün (*green*) → das Grün (*the green*)
Map locations: der Süd(en) (*the south*)	Many trees: die Buche (*the beech*)	Geographic place names: das Europa (*Europe*)
Names of cars: der Audi (*the Audi*)		Infinitives used as nouns (gerunds): schwimmen (*to swim*) → das Schwimmen (*swimming*)
Nationalities and words showing citizenship: der Amerikaner (*the American*)		Young people and animals: das Baby (*the baby*)
Male form occupations: der Arzt (*the doctor*)		

> *Note:* Compound nouns (nouns with two or more nouns in one word) always have the gender of the last noun: **die Polizei** (*the police*) + **der Hund** (*the dog*) = **der Polizeihund** (*the police dog*).

Working without articles

In a few instances in German, you don't use an article in the sentence. First of all, you don't use the indefinite article when you mention someone's profession, nationality, or religion. Here are three examples:

> **Mein Onkel war General bei der Bundeswehr.** (*My uncle was [a] general in the army.*)

> **Sind Sie Australier oder Neuseeländer?** (*Are you [an] Australian or [a] New Zealander?*) Nationalities are nouns in German.

> **Ich glaube, dass sie Lutheranerin ist.** (*I think she's [a] Lutheran.*) Members of a religious affiliation (or an affiliation such as a political party) are nouns in German.

Secondly, just as in English, you don't use the definite article in generalized statements using plural nouns in German. For example: **Bienen sind sehr fleißige Insekten.** (*Bees are very industrious insects.*) But you do use the plural definite article when you're not making a generalization: **Die Bäume haben keine Blätter.** (*The trees have no leaves.*)

Thirdly, names of countries have genders in German, most often **das,** but you generally don't include the definite article, such as in **Viele berühmte Komponisten sind aus Deutschland oder Österreich.** (*Many famous composers are from Germany or Austria.*)

However, a small number of exceptions exist, notably:

> **Die Schweiz gehört nicht zur Europäischen Union.** (*Switzerland doesn't belong to the European Union.*) Note **die,** the feminine definite article.

> **Die Vereinigten Staaten sind die größte Volkswirtschaft der Welt.** (*The United States has the largest economy in the world.*) Note **die,** the plural definite article.

Some other exceptions include **der Irak** (*Irak*), **der Iran** (*Iran*), **die Niederlande** (*the Netherlands*), **die Philippinen** (*the Philippines*), and **die Türkei** (*Turkey*).

Forming plurals

To form plural definite articles in German, **die** (*the* in plural form) is all you need. **Die** corresponds to all three singular definite article forms: **der, die,** and **das.**

Although **die** has a double duty of a singular feminine definite article and a plural definite article for all three genders, you can distinguish between singular and plural. First, find out the difference in noun endings for each feminine noun in its singular form and its plural form. Next, consider the context in the sentence because it may help you see whether you're dealing with a singular or plural form of the noun. Case also enters into the equation; I tell you about case in the later section "Cracking the Cases."

Table 2-3 shows you the five main ways of forming plural nouns in German. There's no hard-and-fast method of knowing which plural ending you need, so try to place high priority on knowing plural forms. Look at some patterns for forming plural nouns (and keep in mind that exceptions may exist):

✔ Feminine nouns with (feminine) suffixes **-heit, -keit,** and **-ung** usually have an **-en** plural ending: **die Möglichkeit** (*the possibility*) → **die Möglichkeiten** (*possibilities*).

✔ Singular nouns ending in **-er** may not have any ending in plural: **das Fenster** (*the window*) → **die Fenster** (*the windows*).

✔ Many nouns have an umlaut in the plural form, including many one-syllable words: **der Kuss** (*the kiss*) → **die Küsse** (*the kisses*); **der Traum** (*the dream*) → **die Träume** (*the dreams*).

✔ Some German nouns are used only in the plural or in the singular: **die Ferien** (*the [often: school] vacation*) is always plural; **die Milch** (*the milk*) is always singular.

Table 2-3	The Five German Plural Groups		
Change Needed	**English Singular and Plural**	**German Singular**	**German Plural**
Add -s	the office(s)	das Büro	die Büros
	the café(s)	das Café	die Cafés
	the boss(es)	der Chef	die Chefs
	the pen(s)	der Kuli	die Kulis
No change, or add umlaut (··)	the computer(s)	der Computer	die Computer
	the window(s)	das Fenster	die Fenster
	the garden(s)	der Garten	die Gärten
	the girl(s)	das Mädchen	die Mädchen
	the father(s)	der Vater	die Väter
Add -e or umlaut (··) + -e	the train station(s)	der Bahnhof	die Banhöfe
	the friend(s) (singular is male)	der Freund	die Freunde
	the problem(s)	das Problem	die Probleme
	the city/cities	die Stadt	die Städte
	the chair(s)	der Stuhl	die Stühle
Add -er or umlaut (··) + -er	the book(s)	das Buch	die Bücher
	the bicycle(s)	das Fahrrad	die Fahrräder
	the house(s)	das Haus	die Häuser
	the child/children	das Kind	die Kinder
	the castle(s)	das Schloss	die Schlösser
Add -n, -en, or -nen	the idea(s)	die Idee	die Ideen
	the boy(s)	der Junge	die Jungen
	the sister(s)	die Schwester	die Schwestern
	the student(s) (female)	die Studentin	die Studentinnen
	the newspaper(s)	die Zeitung	die Zeitungen

Cracking the Cases

German speakers indicate the function of a noun in a sentence mainly by adding endings to any articles or adjectives accompanying that noun (and sometimes to the noun itself). The next sections introduce you to the four German *cases* — the roles nouns can play in a sentence — and illustrate why these cases are so important to proper German grammar.

Identifying the four cases

In a sentence, nouns appear in one of four cases, depending on their role: *nominative* for the subject, *accusative* for the direct object, *dative* for the indirect object, and *genitive* to show possession.

- **Nominative case:** The subject of a sentence is always in the nominative case. As a rule, the subject is the person or thing performing the action of the verb. For example, in the sentence **Der Junge stiehlt eine Wurst** (*The boy steals a sausage*), the boy is the subject of the sentence: He's the one stealing a sausage.

- **Accusative case:** The direct object of the sentence is always in the accusative case. The direct object is the person or thing directly affected by the action of the verb. So in the example sentence introduced in the preceding bullet, *sausage* is the direct object. It's the thing that's being stolen.

- **Dative case:** The indirect object of the sentence is always in the dative case. Think of the indirect object as the person or thing that receives the direct object. Look at the sentence **Der Junge gibt dem Hund die Wurst** (*The boy gives the sausage to the dog*). Here, the dog is the indirect object because the boy gives the sausage to Fido. (The sausage is the direct object, the thing that's being given.)

If a sentence has two objects, one of them is probably an indirect object. If in doubt, try translating the sentence into English: If you can put *to* before one of the nouns, that's the indirect object in the German sentence.

✔ **Genitive case:** The genitive case is used to indicate possession. The person or thing that possesses is in the genitive case. For example, in the phrase **der Hund des Jungen** (*the boy's dog*), the boy possesses the dog, so *the boy* is in the genitive case.

Understanding why cases matter

Case is crucial to understand if you want to communicate properly in German. Why? Because the definite and indefinite articles may change spelling, depending on which case they appear in.

Table 2-4 shows you how the definite articles morph according to which case they're being used in.

Table 2-4	Definite Articles by Case			
Gender	*Nominative*	*Accusative*	*Dative*	*Genitive*
Masculine	der	den	dem	des
Feminine	die	die	der	der
Neuter	das	das	dem	des
Plural	die	die	den	der

The following examples show the masculine definite article **der** with its appropriate endings in the four different cases:

Der Fuchs läuft über die Straße. (*The fox is running across the road.*) **Der** = nominative.

Kaufst du den Computer? (*Are you buying the computer?*) **Den** = accusative.

Ich leihe dem Freund mein Auto. (*I'm lending my car to the friend.*) **Dem** = dative.

Sie lebt in der Wohnung des Freundes. (*She lives in the friend's apartment.*) **Des** = genitive.

Table 2-5 shows you the indefinite article **ein** being put through the paces of the various cases.

Table 2-5		Endings of Ein by Case		
Gender	Nominative	Accusative	Dative	Genitive
Masculine	ein	einen	einem	eines
Feminine	eine	eine	einer	einer
Neuter	ein	ein	einem	eines

The following examples show the indefinite article **ein** with its appropriate masculine endings in the four different cases:

Ein Fuchs läuft über die Straße. (*A fox is running across the road.*) **Ein** = nominative.

Kaufst du einen Computer? (*Are you buying a computer?*) **Einen** = accusative.

Ich leihe einem Freund mein Auto. (*I'm lending my car to a friend.*) **Einem** = dative.

Sie lebt in der Wohnung eines Freundes. (*She lives in a friend's apartment.*) **Eines** = genitive.

Pinch-Hitting with Pronouns

Pronouns need to change spelling/endings according to the role they're playing in a sentence (case) and the noun for which they may be doing the pinch hitting. This section covers the three types of pronouns: personal, demonstrative, and relative pronouns. (Reflexive pronouns are tied to reflexive verbs, so I cover them in Chapter 3.)

Note: One more group of pronouns, called the possessive pronouns — such as **mein** (*my*), **dein** (*your*), **unser** (*our*), and so on — are, technically speaking, classified as adjectives; they have endings that resemble those of descriptive adjectives such as *interesting, tiny,* or *pink.* (See Chapter 5 for more details on possessive adjectives.)

Personalizing with personal pronouns

The personal pronoun family comes in very handy in all kinds of situations when you want to talk (or write) about people, including yourself, without repeating names all the time. You use the nominative case very frequently in most any language, and German is no exception. (See the earlier section "Cracking the Cases" for more on cases.)

With German personal pronouns, the biggest difference is that you have to distinguish among three ways to formulate how to say *you* to your counterpart: **du, ihr,** and **Sie.** Other personal pronouns, such as **ich** and **mich** (*I* and *me*) or **wir** and **uns** (*we* and *us*), bear a closer resemblance to English. *Note:* The genitive case isn't represented among the personal pronouns because it indicates possession; the personal pronoun **mich** (*me*) can represent only a person, not something he or she possesses.

Check out Table 2-6 for the personal pronouns. Notice that *you* and *it* don't change. I've added the distinguishing factors for the three forms **du, ihr,** and **Sie** in abbreviated form: singular = s., plural = pl., informal = inf., formal = form.

Table 2-6	Personal Pronouns	
Nominative (nom.)	*Accusative (acc.)*	*Dative (dat.)*
ich (*I*)	**mich** (*me*)	**mir** (*me*)
du (*you*) (s., inf.)	**dich** (*you*)	**dir** (*you*)
er (*he*)	**ihn** (*him*)	**ihm** (*him*)
sie (*she*)	**sie** (*her*)	**ihr** (*her*)
es (*it*)	**es** (*it*)	**ihm** (*it*)
wir (*we*)	**uns** (*us*)	**uns** (*us*)
ihr (*you*) (pl., inf.)	**euch** (*you*)	**euch** (*you*)
sie (*they*)	**sie** (*them*)	**ihnen** (*them*)
Sie (*you*) (s. or pl., form.)	**Sie** (*you*)	**Ihnen** (*you*)

Relating to relative pronouns

You use relative pronouns (*who, whom, whose, that,* and *which*) to include extra information about a noun or pronoun expressed beforehand. You typically see relative pronouns at the front of a relative clause where they refer back to the noun in the main clause. And what is a *main clause?* It's a sentence fragment that can stand on its own and still make sense.

A *relative clause* is a type of *subordinate clause,* which, as you can probably guess, is the type of sentence fragment that can't stand alone.

Following are the three key points about relative pronouns:

- ✔ **In German, you must use a relative pronoun to connect the main clause and the relative clause.** In English, you don't always have to. For example: **Ist das der Mann, den du liebst?** (*Is that the man [whom, that] you love?*) In this sentence, the main clause is followed by the relative clause, **den du liebst. Den** is the relative pronoun connecting the two parts of the sentence.

- ✔ **You place a comma between the main clause and the relative clause.** Remember that the relative clause begins with the relative pronoun. For example: **Bestellen wir die Pizza, die wir meistens essen.** (*Let's order the pizza that we usually eat.*) In German, you have a comma separating the main clause **Bestellen wir die Pizza** from the relative clause **die wir meistens essen,** which begins with the relative pronoun **die.**

- ✔ **Word order comes into play in relative clauses.** You push the conjugated verb to the end of the clause. For example: **Gestern habe ich eine gute Freundin getroffen, die ich seit Jahren nicht gesehen habe.** (*Yesterday I met a good [female] friend whom I haven't seen for years.*) In the relative clause **die ich seit Jahren nicht gesehen habe,** the verb has two parts: **gesehen,** the past participle, and **habe,** which is the conjugated part of the verb. **Habe** is the last word in the sentence. (For in-depth information on the present perfect verb tense, go to Chapter 7.)

Table 2-7 shows the breakdown of the relative pronouns (*who, whom, whose,* and *that*) by gender and case.

Table 2-7	Relative Pronouns			
Gender/Number of the Noun Being Replaced	**Nominative Case**	**Accusative Case**	**Dative Case**	**Genitive Case**
Masculine (m.)	der	den	dem	dessen
Feminine (f.)	die	die	der	deren
Neuter (n.)	das	das	dem	dessen
Plural (pl.)	die	die	denen	deren

Demonstrating the demonstrative pronouns

You use a demonstrative pronoun when you want to empha-size or point out the pronoun that's replacing a noun. Besides the demonstrative pronouns *he, it, they,* and so on, which are the translations (in parentheses) that you see in Table 2-8, you can also translate these pronouns with the demonstratives *this, that, these,* or *those.* Similar to English, the demonstrative pronoun generally comes at the beginning of a phrase. You use demonstrative pronouns in the nominative case to emphasize the subject or in the accusative case to emphasize the object.

When it comes to demonstrative pronouns, there's just one difference between the nominative case and the accusative case, and that's with the masculine pronouns. **Der** is the nom-inative, and **den** is the accusative case. With the exception of the accusative **den,** you need to know only the gender of the noun that you're replacing — or whether it's plural — and then use that form of the demonstrative pronoun.

Table 2-8	Demonstrative Pronouns	
Gender/Number of the Noun Being Replaced	Nominative Case (for Subjects and Predicate Nouns)	Accusative Case (for Direct Objects)
Masculine (m.)	**der** (*he/it*)	**den** (*him/it*)
Feminine (f.)	**die** (*she/it*)	**die** (*her/it*)
Neuter (n.)	**das** (*it*)	**das** (*it*)
Plural (pl.)	**die** (*they*)	**die** (*them*)

The underlined words in the following examples are the nouns and the demonstrative pronouns that are standing in for the noun to show emphasis:

- **Ist der Flug ausgebucht?** (*Is the flight completely booked?*) **Der Flug** is a masculine singular noun; it's in the nominative case.

  Ja, der ist voll. (*Yes, it's full.*) **Der** is the subject of the sentence, so it's in the nominative case, and it replaces **der Flug,** which is masculine singular. **Der** is the masculine singular demonstrative pronoun in the nominative case.

✔ **Wie findest du die Trauben?** (*How do you like the grapes?*) **Die Trauben** is plural; it's in the accusative case.

Die finde ich herrlich! (*I think they're terrific!*) **Die** is the direct object of the sentence, so it's accusative. **Die** pinch hits for **die Trauben,** which is plural, so you use the plural accusative demonstrative pronoun, **die.**

✔ **Wo hast du den Mantel gekauft?** (*Where did you buy the coat?*) **Den Mantel** is the masculine singular noun **der Mantel,** in the accusative case.

Den habe ich bei Kaufhaus Cloppenburg gekauft. (*I bought it at Cloppenburg department store.*) **Den** is the object of the sentence, and it replaces **den Mantel. Den** is the masculine singular demonstrative pronoun in the accusative case.

✔ **War die Prüfung schwierig?** (*Was the test difficult?*) **Die Prüfung** is a feminine singular noun; it's nominative.

Nein, die war sehr leicht. (*No, it was very easy.*) **Die** is the subject of the sentence, so it's nominative. **Die** replaces **die Prüfung.** It's the feminine singular demonstrative pronoun in the nominative case.

Chapter 3

Handling the Present

- -

In This Chapter

▶ Understanding the types of German verbs in present tense

▶ Choosing the appropriate subject pronoun

▶ Dealing with German present tense verbs and their conjugations

- -

*G*erman uses the present tense in virtually all the same situations that English does. In addition, because German doesn't have a present continuous tense (as in, *What are you thinking?*), you use the present tense in German (as in, *What do you think?*).

In this chapter, you find out how to conjugate regular and irregular verbs and verbs with spelling changes. You also get a grasp of how to use reflexive verbs, prefix verbs, and German subject pronouns.

Classifying Verbs

One way to remember various verb conjugations is to know which category a particular verb falls in. Here are the five possible categories, along with characteristics of the verbs in each one:

> ✔ **Regular verbs:** These verbs have no change in the stem (infinitive minus the -en ending), and their endings are -e, -st, -t, -en, -t, -en, and -en.
>
> ✔ **Verbs with spelling changes:** These verbs have spelling changes in the stem; their endings are the same as those of regular verbs, with some exceptions.

✓ **Irregular verbs:** These verbs have an irregular pattern of conjugation. The two most common are **haben** (*to have*) and **sein** (*to be*).

✓ **Reflexive verbs:** This group of verbs has two parts: the verb and a reflexive pronoun.

✓ **Prefix verbs:** These verbs have a prefix that changes the meaning of the original verb. The three types of prefix verbs are separable-prefix verbs, inseparable-prefix verbs, and dual-prefix verbs.

Selecting Subject Pronouns

You use *subject pronouns* — **ich** (*I*), **du** (*you*), **er** (*he*), **sie** (*she*), **es** (*it*), and so on — to express who or what is carrying out the action or idea of a verb. They refer to the noun without naming it. (For more information on pronouns, check out Chapters 1 and 2.) Table 3-1 shows you the breakdown of subject pronouns in German and English.

Table 3-1	Subject Pronouns	
Person	*Singular*	*Plural*
First	**ich** (*I*)	**wir** (*we*)
Second (familiar)	**du** (*you*)	**ihr** (*you*)
Third	**er** (*he, it*)	**sie** (*they*)
	sie (*she, it*)	
	es (*it*)	
Second (formal)	**Sie** (*you;* both singular and plural)	

Here's a closer look at the three persons:

✓ **First person:** The one(s) speaking: **ich** (*I*) or **wir** (*we*).

✓ **Second person:** The one(s) spoken *to:* **du, ihr, Sie.** All three mean *you* in English; **du** is the singular, familiar form, which you'd use with a friend; **ihr** is the plural, familiar form, which you'd use with a group of friends; and **Sie** is the formal form, whether singular or plural, which you'd use with people you're not on a first-name basis with.

✔ **Third person:** Who or what is spoken *about:* **er** (*he, it*), **sie** (*she, it*), or **es** (*it*); **sie** (*they*). If you're talking about an inanimate object (*it*), the choice among **er, sie,** and **es** depends on the gender of the noun. I explain how to determine a noun's gender in Chapter 2.

Addressing someone formally or informally

Use **Sie,** which is always capitalized, to speak to one or more people with whom you have a more distant, formal relationship. **Sie** is appropriate in the following situations:

✔ When you aren't sure about whether **du/ihr** or **Sie** is correct

✔ When you're not yet on a first-name basis with someone (for example, using Herr Kuhnagel or Frau Zitzelsberger, not Sigmund or Hildegard)

✔ When you're talking to adults you don't know well

✔ In business or at your place of work

✔ In public situations to a person in uniform (police officer, airport official, and other such individuals)

Use **du** when you talk to one person (or animal) in an informal way, and use **ihr,** the plural version of **du,** to address more than one person (or animal) informally. An informal pronoun is appropriate in these instances:

✔ When a German speaker invites you to use **du**

✔ For talking to a relative or a close friend

✔ For addressing children and teens younger than 16 or so

✔ When you talk to pets

You may hear **du** among close working colleagues, students, members of a sports team, or people hiking in the mountains, but unless someone asks you, **"Wollen wir uns duzen?"** (*Shall we say **du** to each other?*), try to stick with **Sie.**

Unraveling sie, sie, and Sie

Take a moment to be sure you know how to unravel the three-some tangle of subject pronouns. Refer to Table 3-1, and you find the Three Musketeers, **sie** (*she*), **sie** (*they*), and **Sie** (*you*), lurking in their separate boxes. Here's what to watch:

- ✔ **Conjugation:** When **sie** means *she,* its verb form is distinct; in the present tense, the conjugated verb usually ends in **-t.** When **sie/Sie** means *they* or *you,* the present-tense verb ends in **-en.**

- ✔ **Capitalization:** The *they* and *you* forms of **sie/Sie** have identical conjugations, but only the *you* version, which is formal, is capitalized.

The following examples show you how to figure out which one to use and when:

Wo wohnt sie? (*Where does she live?*) The verb is in third-person singular form.

Wo wohnen sie? (*Where do they live?*) The verb is in third-person plural form, and **sie** isn't capitalized.

Wo wohnen Sie? (*Where do you live?*) The verb is in second-person plural form (which is identical to the third-person plural form), and **Sie** is capitalized.

Expressing Yourself in the Present Tense

Most German verbs are *regular* in the present tense, meaning they follow a standard pattern of conjugation. Others follow a more irregular conjugation pattern, and some require you to change the spelling of the verb. Then you have the reflexive verbs and prefix verbs. The following sections explain how to work with the various verb types so you can say just about anything you want in that most versatile of German tenses, the present tense.

Looking at regular verbs

To conjugate a regular verb in the present tense, you take the stem — which is almost always the result of lopping off **-en** from the *infinitive* (or not-yet-conjugated) form of the verb — and add the appropriate ending to the stem. The endings are **-e, -st, -t, -en, -t, -en,** and **-en.**

The following verb table shows how to conjugate the verb **kommen** (*to come*). I've simply added the present-tense endings, marked in bold, onto the stem **komm-.**

kommen (*to come*)	
ich komm**e**	wir komm**en**
du komm**st**	ihr komm**t**
er/sie/es komm**t**	sie komm**en**
Sie komm**en**	
Er **kommt** aus Irland. (*He comes from Ireland.*)	

If the verb stem ends in **-d** or **-t,** place an **e** in front of the verb endings **-st** and **-t.** The following table shows you how to conjugate a regular verb like **arbeiten** (*to work*) in the present tense. The endings are marked in bold.

arbeiten (*to work*)	
ich arbeit**e**	wir arbeit**en**
du arbeit**est**	ihr arbeit**et**
er/sie/es arbeit**et**	sie arbeit**en**
Sie arbeit**en**	
Du **arbeitest** sehr schnell. (*You work very fast.*)	

With a few verbs that don't have an **-en** infinitive ending, notably **wandern** (*to hike*) and **tun** (*to do*), drop **-n** from the infinitive and add only **-n** to the following:

✔ First-person plural form: **wir wandern** (*we hike*) and **wir tun** (*we do*)

✔ Third-person plural form: **sie wandern** (*they hike*) and **sie tun** (*they do*)

✔ Formal second-person singular and plural form: **Sie wandern** (*you hike*) and **Sie tun** (*you do*)

Following are other common German verbs that conjugate according to the previous present-tense rules. Some verbs on the following list are irregular in other verb tenses, even though they follow the regular present-tense rules. These verbs have the information *irregular* or *mixed* in parentheses shown after the verb.

✔ **arbeiten** (*to work*)

✔ **bringen** (*to bring*)

✔ **finden** (*to find, have an opinion*) (mixed)

✔ **gehen** (*to go, walk*) (irregular)

✔ **heißen** (*to be called, named*) (irregular)

✔ **kaufen** (*to buy*) (irregular)

✔ **kennen** (*to know [a person]*)

✔ **kommen** (*to come*)

✔ **kosten** (*to cost*) (irregular)

✔ **lernen** (*to learn*)

✔ **reisen** (*to travel*)

✔ **sagen** (*to say*)

✔ **schreiben** (*to write*)

✔ **spielen** (*to play [a game, cards]*)

✔ **wandern** (*to hike, wander*)

✔ **wohnen** (*to live*)

Remembering verbs with spelling changes

Certain verbs have spelling changes. They're technically classified as verbs with stem-vowel changes because the vowel(s) in the stem changes when you conjugate the verb. (The stem is the part of the infinitive left after you slice off the **-en** ending: **Sprechen** [*to speak*] is the infinitive, and **sprech-** is the stem.)

The stem-vowel changes take place in the **du** and **er/sie/es** forms (and in one verb type, the **ich** form).

The next tables show the five types of stem-vowel changes, along with the additional changes in **nehmen** (*to take*) and **wissen** (*to know as a fact*) groups. In these tables, only the stem-vowel changing verb forms are in bold.

fahren (*to drive*): a→ä	
ich fahre	wir fahren
du **fährst**	ihr fahrt
er/sie/es **fährt**	sie fahren
Sie fahren	
Du **fährst** sehr vorsichtig. (*You drive very carefully.*)	

Other **a→ä** verbs include **backen** (*to bake*), **fallen** (*to fall*), **gefallen** (*to like, enjoy*), **halten** (*to stop, think about*), **schlafen** (*to sleep*), **tragen** (*to carry, wear*), **waschen** (*to wash*). A very small group has a slightly different stem-vowel change: **au→äu**. This group includes **laufen** (*to run*).

sprechen (*to speak*): e→i	
ich spreche	wir sprechen
du **sprichst**	ihr sprecht
er/sie/es **spricht**	sie sprechen
Sie sprechen	
Adrienne **spricht** fließend Englisch, Deutsch, und Französisch. (*Adrienne speaks fluent English, German, and French.*)	

Here are some other **e→i** verbs: **essen** (*to eat*), **geben** (*to give*), **helfen** (*to help*), **vergessen** (*to forget*).

lesen (*to read*): e→ie	
ich lese	wir lesen
du **liest**	ihr lest
er/sie/es **liest**	sie lesen
Sie lesen	
Das Kind **liest** schon Romane. (*The child already reads novels.*)	

Sehen (*to see*) is also an **e→ie** verb.

nehmen (*to take*): e→i, hm→mm	
ich nehme	wir nehmen
du **nimmst**	ihr nehmt
er/sie/es **nimmt**	sie nehmen
Sie nehmen	
Du **nimmst** zu viele Kekse! (*You're taking too many cookies!*)	

wissen (*to know as a fact*): i→ei	
ich **weiß**	wir wissen
du **weißt**	ihr wisst
er/sie/es **weiß**	sie wissen
Sie wissen	
Weißt du, wer das ist? (*Do you know who that is?*)	

Dealing with the irregulars

The two common verbs **haben** (*to have*) and **sein** (*to be*), are irregular. The following sections show you the basics you need to know in order to use these verbs in the present tense.

Haben: Let me have it

Look at the conjugation of **haben** in the present tense. Notice that the verb actually has only two irregular verb forms: **du hast** and **er/sie/es hat.**

haben (*to have*)	
ich **habe**	wir **haben**
du **hast**	ihr **habt**
er/sie/es **hat**	sie **haben**
Sie **haben**	
Sie **hat** eine grosse Familie. (*She has a large family.*)	

German has many expressions that involve the verb *to have*. Some common uses of **haben** are

- ✔ **Expressing likes with haben and the adverb gern: Gern** means *gladly, with pleasure* when you use it alone. **Hast du klassische Musik gern?** (*Do you like classical music?*)

- ✔ **Talking about your birthday:** You say, **Ich habe am achten Oktober Geburtstag.** (*My birthday is on the eighth of October.*)

- ✔ **With expressions that describe a physical condition, an emotional condition, or a state of being:** Five common expressions are **Angst haben** (*to be afraid*), **Durst haben** (*to be thirsty*), **Glück haben** (*to be lucky, fortunate*), **Hunger haben** (*to be hungry*), and **Recht haben** (*to be right*):

    Ich habe Angst vor Haifische. (*I'm afraid of sharks.*)

    Haben Sie Durst? (*Are you thirsty?*)

    Du hast viel Glück. (*You're very lucky.*)

    Wir haben keinen Hunger. (*We're not hungry.*)

    Der Lehrer hat Recht. (*The teacher is right.*)

Sein: To be or not to be

Look at the conjugation of **sein** (*to be*) in the present tense. Notice that all the verb forms are irregular, although **wir sind, sie sind,** and **Sie sind** are identical.

sein (*to be*)	
ich **bin**	wir **sind**
du **bist**	ihr **seid**
er/sie/es **ist**	sie **sind**
Sie **sind**	
Sind Sie Herr Rasch? (*Are you Mr. Rasch?*)	

German uses the verb **sein** (*to be*) in a great number of ways. Here's how you can use **sein:**

✔ **With an adjective:** This way is the most common:

Du bist sehr lustig. (*You're very funny.*)

Mein Sohn ist nicht musikalisch. (*My son is not musical.*)

✔ **With an adjective plus a noun or pronoun in the dative case:** A couple of common expressions are

Mir ist kalt/warm. (*I'm cold/warm.*) **Mir** is the dative case of the pronoun **ich.**

Ihm ist schlecht/übel. (*He's feeling sick/sick to his stomach.*) **Ihm** is the dative case of the pronoun **er.**

✔ **With an adverb:**

Wir sind morgen nicht hier. (*We're not here tomorrow.*)

Sie ist dort. (*She's there.*)

✔ **With nouns:**

Sind Sie Kanadier? (*Are you a Canadian?*)

Ich bin Bauingenieur. (*I'm a civil engineer.*)

Mirroring with reflexive verbs

Reflexive verbs have a subject that carries out an action directed at itself. A German reflexive verb has two elements: the verb and its accompanying reflexive pronoun. Both English and German have two cases of reflexive pronouns: accusative and dative.

Table 3-2 shows the reflexive pronouns together with their translations. The corresponding nominative pronouns are in the left-hand column. Here's the key to the abbreviations: s. = singular, pl. = plural, inf. = informal, and form. = formal.

Table 3-2	Reflexive Pronouns	
Nominative (nom.) Pronouns for Reference	*Accusative (acc.)*	*Dative (dat.)*
ich (*I*)	**mich** (*myself*)	**mir** (*myself*)
du (*you*) (s.; inf.)	**dich** (*yourself*)	**dir** (*yourself*)

Nominative (nom.) Pronouns for Reference	Accusative (acc.)	Dative (dat.)
er/sie/es (*he/she/it*)	**sich** (*himself/herself/ itself*)	**sich** (*himself/herself/ itself*)
wir (*we*)	**uns** (*ourselves*)	**uns** (*ourselves*)
ihr (*you*) (pl.; inf.)	**euch** (*yourselves*)	**euch** (*yourselves*)
sie (*they*)	**sich** (*themselves*)	**sich** (*themselves*)
Sie (*you*) (s. or pl.; form.)	**sich** (*yourself* or *yourselves*)	**sich** (*yourself* or *yourselves*)

The verbs that use a dative reflexive pronoun appear in sentences that have a separate direct object; the verbs that use an accusative reflexive pronoun have no separate direct object in the sentence. Check out the following examples:

Ich fühle mich viel besser. (*I feel/I'm feeling much better.*) **Mich** (*myself*) is the accusative form of the reflexive pronoun; it's the direct object that refers back to the subject performing the action of the verb **fühlen.**

Ich ziehe mir eine Jeans an. (*I put on/I'm putting on a pair of jeans.*) **Mir** is the dative form of the reflexive pronoun; **eine Jeans** is the direct object (accusative case) in the sentence.

Word order plays an important role in sentence construction with reflexive pronouns. Keep the following important points in mind:

✔ In a statement, the reflexive pronoun immediately follows the conjugated verb; **sich** comes right after **freuen** in this example: **Die Touristen freuen sich auf die Reise.** (*The tourists are looking forward to the trip.*)

✔ In a question, if the subject is a pronoun (**ihr** [*you*]), then you place the reflexive pronoun (**euch** [*you*]) directly after it. For example: **Erkältet ihr euch oft?** (*Do you often catch colds?*)

In German, you frequently find the reflexive in references to parts of the body. These verbs often describe what you do to yourself when you're in the bathroom. For example, shaving (**sich rasieren** [*to shave oneself*]) is a reflexive verb.

Table 3-3 lists some reflexive verbs, many of which have to do with daily routine, especially personal hygiene.

Table 3-3	Reflexive Verbs: The Daily Routine
German Expression	*English Equivalent*
sich anziehen (acc.)	*to get dressed*
sich (das Hemd) anziehen (dat.)	*to put on (one's shirt)*
sich beeilen (acc.)	*to hurry (up)*
sich duschen (acc.)	*to take a shower*
sich freuen auf (den Tag) (acc.)	*to look forward to (the day)*
sich die Zähne putzen (dat.)	*to brush/clean one's teeth*
sich rasieren (acc.)	*to shave oneself*
sich (das Gesicht) rasieren (dat.)	*to shave (one's face)*
sich die Haare waschen (dat.)	*to wash (one's hair)*
sich die Hände waschen (dat.)	*to wash (one's hands)*

Sorting out prefix verbs

In English, verbs such as *get up* and *work out* are called *two-part* or *phrasal verbs*. Their German counterparts are called *separable-* and *inseparable-prefix verbs*. The German *prefix* (which corresponds to the second part of a two-part verb in English) may stand for a preposition, such as *up,* or an adverb, such as *away*. In both English and German, the prefix alters the meaning of the original verb, sometimes only slightly, sometimes radically.

The following sections show you how to use the three types of prefix verbs in the present tense: separable-prefix verbs, inseparable-prefix verbs, and dual-prefix verbs.

Simplifying separable-prefix verbs

The verb and the prefix can split up in *separable-prefix verbs*. This group of prefix verbs is the largest because it has the largest number of prefixes as well as the largest number of verbs that connect with these prefixes.

With separable-prefix verbs in the present tense, keep the following two points in mind:

- The prefix — such as **fest-** in **festhalten** (*to hold on*) — goes to the end of the sentence. In spoken German, you stress the prefix.

- The verb itself, which is the part you conjugate, is generally in second position in the sentence, as in, **Ich halte mich fest.** (*I'm holding on tight.*)

Table 3-4 shows separable prefixes, their English meanings, and one or two verbs that use the prefix. These verbs are pretty common, so you're likely to encounter many of them.

Table 3-4   Separable Prefixes and Verb Combinations

Prefix	English Definition	Example Verb	English Equivalent
ab-	from	abbrechen	to break away, stop
		abschaffen	to do away with
an-	at, to, on	anfangen	to begin, start
		anrufen	to phone
auf-	on, out, up	aufgeben	to give up, check (bags)
aus-	from, out	ausbilden	to train, educate
		ausfallen	to cancel, fall out (hair)
bei-	with, along	beitreten	to join, enter into (a pact)
da-	there	dableiben	to stay behind
ein-	in, into, down	einkaufen	to go shopping, to buy
		einladen	to invite
entgegen-	against, toward	entgegenkommen	to approach, accommodate
fest-	fixed	festhalten	to hold on, keep hold of

(continued)

Table 3-4 *(continued)*

Prefix	English Definition	Example Verb	English Equivalent
fort-	onward, away	fortbilden	to continue education
		fortführen	to carry on, continue
gegenüber-	across from	gegenüberstehen	to be opposite, face
gleich-	equal	gleichstellen	to treat as equal
her-	from, here	herstellen	to manufacture, establish
hin-	to, toward, there	hinfahren	to drive there, go there
hinzu-	in addition	hinzufügen	to add (details), enclose
kennen-	know	kennenlernen	to get to know, meet
los-	start, away	losbrechen	to break off
		losfahren	to drive off
mit-	along, with	mitarbeiten	to collaborate
		mitteilen	to inform (someone)
nach-	after, copy	nachahmen	to imitate
statt-	no equivalent	stattfinden	to take place (event)
vor-	before	vorbereiten	to prepare
weg-	away, off	wegbleiben	to stay away
zu-	shut, to, upon	zulassen	to authorize, license
zurück-	back	zurückzahlen	to pay back
zusammen-	together	zusammenarbeiten	to work together

Investigating inseparable-prefix verbs

The verb and prefix stay together in *inseparable-prefix verbs.* The good news is that many of these verbs are common German verbs. In addition, some equivalent verbs in English have the same prefix.

The following points define inseparable-prefix verbs:

✔ You don't stress the prefix in spoken German.

✔ The prefix alters the original meaning of the verb.

✔ The prefix sticks with the verb stem in all tenses.

Look at these example sentences:

> **Ich verspreche dir einen Rosengarten.** (*I promise you a rose garden.*) The verb is **versprechen** (*to promise*).

> **Verfahren sich viele Touristen in der Stadt?** (*Do many tourists get lost in the city?*) The verb **verfahren** means *to get lost.* In yes/no questions, the verb is at the beginning of the question.

Table 3-5 lists inseparable prefixes, their English meanings, and one or two verbs that use the prefix.

Table 3-5 Inseparable Prefixes and Verb Combinations

Prefix	English Definition	Example Verb	English Equivalent
be-	similar to English prefix *be-*	**sich befinden** (reflexive)	*to be located*
		bekommen	*to get*
emp-	no equivalent	**empfehlen**	*to recommend*
		empfinden	*to feel*
ent-	similar to English prefixes *de-* and *dis-*	**entbehren**	*to do without*
		entdecken	*to discover*

(continued)

Table 3-5 *(continued)*

Prefix	English Definition	Example Verb	English Equivalent
er-	sometimes no equivalent, sometimes similar to the English prefix *re-* or the meaning of *fatal*	erklären	to explain, declare
		ertrinken	to drown
ge-	no equivalent	gebrauchen	to use, make use of
		gefallen	to like
miss-	similar to English prefix *mis-*	missbrauchen	to misuse, abuse
		missverstehen	to misunderstand
ver-	similar to English prefix *for-*	verbieten	to forbid
		vergessen	to forget
ver-	*(go) awry*	sich verfahren (reflexive)	to get lost
ver-	*away, lose*	verlassen	to leave, abandon
ver-	no equivalent	vergrößern	to enlarge
		versprechen	to promise
voll-	*complete*	vollenden	to complete, come to an end
zer-	*completely (ruin)*	zerbrechen	to shatter
		zerstören	to destroy

Dealing with dual-prefix verbs

The *dual-prefix verbs* are characterized by having a prefix that can combine to make both separable-prefix verbs and inseparable-prefix verbs. The list of these prefixes is short.

Follow these guidelines to help you remember dual-prefix verbs:

✔ Some dual prefixes are mainly separable, and others are mainly inseparable. For example, **um-** is a prefix that is mainly separable, and **über-** is a prefix that is mainly inseparable.

✔ Some dual-prefix verbs are both separable and inseparable. The verb in its literal meaning has a separable prefix, such as with **Die Fähre setzt uns ans andere Ufer über** (*The ferry is taking us across to the other bank [side]*).

The verb in its figurative meaning has an inseparable prefix, such as with **Sie übersetzt sehr schnell** (*She translates very quickly*).

Table 3-6 is a list of dual-prefix verbs indicating whether they're separable- or inseparable-prefix verbs, and the English verb equivalents.

Table 3-6 Dual Prefixes and Verb Combinations

Prefix	English Definition	Example Verb	English Equivalent
durch- (usually sep.)	*through*	**durchbringen** (sep.)	*to get through*
		durchfahren (sep.)	*to drive through*
hinter-	*behind*	**hinterlassen** (sep.)	*to let someone go behind*
		hinterlassen (insep.)	*to leave, bequeath*
über- (usually insep.)	*over, across*	**übernachten** (insep.)	*to sleep (in a hotel and such)*
		übersetzen (insep.)	*to translate*
		übersetzen (sep.)	*to ferry across*
um- (usually sep.)	*around*	**umsteigen** (sep.)	*to change (trains)*
		umziehen (sep.)	*to move, change (clothes)*

(continued)

Table 3-6 *(continued)*

Prefix	English Definition	Example Verb	English Equivalent
unter-	down, under	unterbrechen (insep.)	to interrupt, disconnect
		untergehen (sep.)	to sink, go down
wider- (usually insep.)	against (similar to English prefix *re-*)	widerrufen (insep.)	to recall (product)
		widersprechen (insep.)	to contradict
wieder-	again	wiederholen (sep.)	to get back
		wiederholen (insep.)	to repeat

Comparison of Equals/Nonequals	English Equivalent	Example Sentence	English Equivalent
halb so ... wie ...	*half as ... as ...*	Das Ergebnis war nur **halb so** schlimm **wie** wir erwarteten.	*The result was only half as bad as we expected.*
(nicht) so ... wie ...	*(not) as ... as ...*	Ich bin **(nicht) so** stark **wie** ich dachte.	*I'm not as strong as I thought.*
je ... , desto ... (comparative words follow **je ... , desto ...**)	*the ... -er, the ... -er* (adjectives or adverbs in comparative form)	**Je mehr** Sie lesen, **desto besser** informiert werden Sie. (***Note:*** The word order is different in English.)	*The more you read, the better informed you'll be.*

Your Personal Preposition Primer

Prepositions are small words that indicate the relationship between a noun, which is the object of the preposition, and another word or words in the sentence. The following section deal with how case plays a role in using prepositions, as well as how two-way prepositions and preposition combinations work.

Looking at the role of cases in prepositions

As with other German words such as nouns, adjectives, and verbs, prepositions need to be understood together with the other trappings of language. A lowly two-letter preposition like **in** (*in, into, to*) has so much power that it forces the noun and other words it connects with to take the same case endings. The preposition doesn't change; it *tells* the others to follow the case of that preposition.

The three cases that prepositions identify with are accusative, dative, and genitive. *Note:* Some prepositions are two-timers; they may use accusative or dative case, depending on meaning. The following examples show all four groups of prepositions. (For the basics of case, see Chapter 2.)

✔ Accusative preposition **durch: Mein Hund Bello läuft gern durch den Wald.** (*My dog Bello likes to run through the woods.*) The phrase is **durch den Wald** (*through the woods*). **Der Wald** in accusative case is **den Wald.**

✔ Dative preposition **mit: Ich laufe gern mit ihm (Bello).** (*I like to run with him.*) The phrase is **mit ihm** (*with him*). **Ihm** is the dative case form of the personal pronoun **er.**

✔ Genitive preposition **während: Während des Winters bleiben Bello und ich oft zu Hause.** (*During the winter, Bello and I often stay at home.*) The phrase is **während des Winters** (*during the winter*). Because **während** is a genitive preposition, **der Winter** in nominative case changes to **des Winters** in genitive case.

✔ Accusative/dative preposition **auf: Meistens liege ich allein auf der Couch, aber manchmal springt Bello auf die Couch.** (*I usually lie on the couch alone, but sometimes he jumps onto the couch.*) **Auf der Couch** (*on the couch*) is dative case; **auf die Couch** (*onto the couch*) is accusative case.

Prepositions that can be either accusative or dative work like this: When the preposition uses the accusative case, it generally shows the motion of something, whereas when the preposition uses the dative case, it indicates location.

Connecting with accusative prepositions

Accusative prepositions express movement, opposition to something, and acts of excluding or receiving. The small band of accusative prepositions, which are strictly linked to the accusative case, includes **bis, durch, für, gegen, ohne,** and **um.** Look in Table 5-7 for a list of these prepositions, their English equivalents, and a sample phrase.

Table 5-7   Accusative Prepositions

Preposition	English Equivalent(s)	Sample Phrases	English Equivalent
bis	*till, until* (also: conjunction *until*)	**bis nächsten Sonntag**	*until next Sunday*

Preposition	English Equivalent(s)	Sample Phrases	English Equivalent
durch	*through, by*	**durch die Stadt (jemanden)**	*through the city*
		durch einen Freund kennen-lernen	*meet (someone) through a friend*
für	*for*	**für Sie**	*for you*
		für meine Freunde	*for my friends*
gegen	*against, for*	**gegen die Regeln**	*against the rules*
		etwas gegen Kopfschmerzen nehmen	*take something for a headache*
ohne	*without*	**ohne mich**	*without me*
		ohne Herrn Adler	*without Herr Adler*
um	*around, for, at*	**um das Haus**	*around the house*
		Ich bewerbe mich um die Stelle.	*I'm applying for the job.*

To form phrases with accusative prepositions, start with the preposition and add the information that the preposition is linking to the rest of the sentence — the preposition's object (noun) and any modifiers. If necessary, change the endings of any articles, pronouns, adjectives, and nouns following the preposition to the accusative case. Here's what needs to change:

✔ Some definite articles change. The definite articles are easy because the only change is **der** → **den**. **Die** (feminine and plural) and **das** don't change. (See Chapter 2 for the lowdown on definite articles.)

✔ The accusative prepositions build some contractions: **durch + das = durchs; für + das = fürs; um + das = ums.**

In spoken, colloquial German, these contractions are very common.

✔ Most of the pronouns change. The personal pronouns in accusative (direct object) case are **mich** (*me*), **dich** (*you*), **ihn/sie/es** (*him/her/it*), **uns** (*us*), **euch** (*you*), **sie** (*them*), and **Sie** (*you*).

✔ Adjectives may or may not undergo an ending change.

✔ A few nouns undergo an ending change. (See Chapter 1 for more on nouns.)

The following example sentences show the role of case and some spelling changes that take place when you use German prepositions:

> **Sammy das Stinktier sitzt ganz allein, ohne seine Freunde.** (*Sammy the skunk is sitting all alone without his friends.*) The preposition **ohne** is followed by **seine Freunde;** both words have accusative plural endings.

> **Dann läuft er durch den Garten der Familie Finkenhuber.** (*Then he runs through the Finkenhuber's garden.*) The preposition **durch** (*through* in this context) indicates movement; **den Garten** is the masculine singular form of **der Garten** in the accusative case.

> **Sammy läuft um den Hund Bello und . . . psst!** (*Sammy runs around Bello the dog and . . . psst!*) The preposition **um** (*around*) indicates movement; **den Hund** is the masculine singular form of **der Hund** in the accusative case.

Working with dative prepositions

Dative prepositions include some heavy hitters. Most dative prepositions express relationships of time (when), motion (where to), and location (where). Some have surprising variations in meaning. Table 5-8 shows eight dative prepositions that are always followed by the dative, their English equivalents, and some sample phrases for each.

Table 5-8		Dative Prepositions	
Preposition	*English Equivalent(s)*	*Sample Phrases*	*English Equivalent*
aus	*from, out of*	**aus den USA**	*from the U.S.A.*
		aus der Arbeit	*from/out of work*

Preposition	English Equivalent(s)	Sample Phrases	English Equivalent
außer	besides, except for	außer uns	besides/except for us
		außer den Kindern	except for the children
bei	at (a home of, a place of business), near, with	bei Katharina	at Katharina's (place)
		bei der Straße	near the street
		Es ist anders bei mir.	It's different with me.
mit	with, by (means of transportation)	mit dem Hund	with the dog
		mit dem Zug	by train
nach	after, past, to	nach einer Stunde	after an hour
		Es ist fünf nach vier.	It's five past four.
		nach Moskau (no article for cities and countries in German)	to Moscow
seit	for, since	seit zwanzig Jahren	for 20 years
		seit dem Krieg	since the war
von	by, from, of	von einem deutschen Maler	by a German artist (created by someone)
		ein Geschenk von dir	a present from you
		am Ende vom Film	at the end of the movie
zu	to (with people and certain places)	zur Universität	to the university
		Was gibt's zum Abendessen?	What's for dinner?

To form phrases with dative prepositions, start with the preposition and add the information that the preposition connects to the rest of the sentence (the object of the preposition and any articles or adverbs that modify it). Change the endings of any articles, pronouns, adjectives, and nouns following the prepositions — if necessary — to the dative case. Here's what needs to change:

> ✔ The definite articles change like this (see Chapter 2 for definite articles): **der** → **dem; die** → **der** (feminine); **das** → **dem; die** → **den** (plural).
>
> **Note:** Not all prepositional phrases need an article (**dem, einen,** and so on) with the noun; these are generally fixed expressions, such as clock times (**es ist Viertel nach acht** [*it's quarter past eight*]) or other types (**zu Hause** [*at home*]).
>
> ✔ The contractions that dative prepositions build are **bei + dem = beim; von + dem = vom; zu + dem = zum; zu + der = zur.** In spoken, colloquial German, these contractions are very common.
>
> ✔ All the pronouns change. The personal pronouns in dative case are **mir** (*me*), **dir** (*you*), **ihm/ihr/ihm** (*him/her/it*), **uns** (*us*), **euch** (*you*), **ihnen** (*them*), and **Ihnen** (*you*). (See Chapter 2 for pronouns.)
>
> ✔ Adjectives may or may not undergo an ending change.
>
> ✔ A few nouns undergo an ending change. (See Chapter 2 for more on nouns.)

The following conversation shows how four of the dative prepositions — **bei, zu, seit,** and **mit** — perform in sentences:

> **Essen wir heute Abend bei dir?** (*Shall we have dinner at your place tonight?*) **Bei** is a true chameleon in respect to meanings. Here, take **bei,** add the dative pronoun **dir,** and presto! — **bei dir** = *at your place.*
>
> **Nein, ich möchte lieber zum Restaurant um die Ecke gehen.** (*No, I'd rather go to the restaurant around the corner.*) The contraction of **zu + dem = zum.**
>
> **Luigis? Es ist seit einem Monat geschlossen.** (*Luigi's? It's been closed for a month.*)
>
> **Wichtig ist nur, dass ich mit dir esse.** (*It's only important that I eat with you.*)

Handling genitive prepositions

The *genitive prepositions* describe duration of time, reasons for something, or opposition to something. Table 5-9 shows the six most common genitive prepositions, their English equivalents, and sample phrases.

Note: Especially in spoken German, but also in written German, using the dative personal pronouns with genitive prepositions is common; for example, **wegen mir** (*because of me*) or **statt dir** (*instead of you*). In spoken German, some genitive prepositions — **anstatt/statt, trotz, wegen,** and **während** — are typically used with the dative case. This is especially true in **Bayern, Österreich, und die Schweiz** (*Bavaria, Austria, and Switzerland*). **Während** uses dative case less frequently in colloquial German than the other three.

Table 5-9	Genitive Prepositions		
Preposition	*English Equivalent(s)*	*Sample Phrases*	*English Equivalent*
(an)statt (no difference between **anstatt** and **statt**)	*instead of*	**(an)statt meines Autos**	*instead of my car*
außerhalb	*outside of*	**außerhalb des Hauses**	*outside of the house*
innerhalb	*inside of*	**innerhalb der Firma**	*within the company*
trotz	*in spite of, despite*	**trotz des Wetters**	*despite the weather*
		trotz des Lärms or Laermes	*in spite of the noise*
während	*during*	**während des Tages**	*during the day*
wegen	*because of, on account of*	**wegen der Kosten**	*on account of the costs*

To form genitive prepositional phrases, begin with the preposition and then add the information that the preposition links to the rest of the sentence. You need to change the endings of any articles, pronouns, adjectives, and nouns following the prepositions — if necessary — so they're also in the genitive case.

Wegen der Hitze gehen wir nicht spazieren. (*We're not going for a walk because of the heat.*) **Die Hitze** in nominative case becomes **der Hitze** in genitive case.

Während des Winters bleiben wir meistens zu Hause. (*We usually stay at home during the winter.*) **Der Winter** in nominative case becomes **des Winters** in genitive case.

Tackling two-way prepositions

Nine prepositions can use either accusative or dative case, depending on meaning. The prepositions in this group are in the accusative case when they describe movement and in the dative case when they describe location.

To determine whether you need to use a two-way preposition in accusative or dative case, visualize what you want to say. Imagine the difference between a cat lying *on* the table — **eine Katze liegt auf dem Tisch** (location = dative case) — and a cat jumping *onto* the table — **eine Katz springt auf den Tisch** (movement = accusative case).

Table 5-10 shows the two-way prepositions, their English equivalents, and a sample phrase for each with the English translation. Because there's no present continuous in German, the present tense (*the mouse runs*) or the present continuous (*the mouse is running*), or both, may be logical translations.

Table 5-10		Two-Way Prepositions	
Preposition	*English Equivalent(s)*	*Accusative Example*	*Dative Example*
an	*at, on* (referring to a vertical surface), *to*	**Die Katze geht ans (an + das) Fenster.** (*The cat walks to the window.*)	**Die Katze sitzt am Fenster.** (*The cat is sitting at the window.*)
auf	*On* (referring to a horizontal surface), *onto, to*	**Die Katze springt auf den Tisch.** (*The cat jumps onto the table.*)	**Die Katze steht auf dem Tisch.** (*The cat is standing on the table.*)

Preposition	English Equivalent(s)	Accusative Example	Dative Example
hinter	behind, to the back of	**Die Katze geht hinter die Couch.** (The cat is going behind the couch.)	**Die Katze sitzt hinter der Couch.** (The cat is sitting behind the couch.)
in	in, into, to	**Die Katze läuft in die Küche.** (The cat is running into the kitchen.)	**Die Katze ist in der Küche.** (The cat is in the kitchen.)
neben	beside, next to	**Der Hund legt sich neben die Katze hin.** (The dog lays itself down next to the cat.)	**Die Katze liegt neben dem Hund.** (The cat is lying next to the dog.)
über	above, over	**Eine Maus läuft über den Teppich.** (A mouse is running over the carpet.)	**Eine Lampe hängt über dem Tisch.** (A lamp is hanging over the table.)
unter	under, underneath	**Die Maus läuft unter den Teppich.** (The mouse runs under the carpet.)	**Der Teppich liegt unter dem Tisch.** (The carpet is lying under the table.)
vor	in front of	**Die Maus läuft vor die Katze.** (The mouse is running in front of the cat.)	**Der Hund sitzt vor dem Fernseher.** (The dog is sitting in front of the TV.)
zwischen	between	**Die Katze legt sich zwischen die Pfoten des Hundes.** (The cat lies down between the dog's paws.)	**Der Hund steht zwischen der Maus und der Katze.** (The dog is standing between the mouse and the cat.)

To form phrases with two-way prepositions, follow the guidelines I describe in the earlier sections "Connecting with accusative prepositions" and "Working with dative prepositions."

 Some two-way prepositions combine with articles to make contractions. These contractions are mostly used in spoken, colloquial German: **an + das = ans; an + dem = am; auf + das = aufs; in + das = ins; in + dem = im.** Other contractions that aren't as frequently used as contractions with **das** and **dem** include **hinters, hinterm, übers, überm, unters, unterm, vors,** and **vorm.** You may encounter these contractions in spoken language.

The following examples clarify how to form and use two-way prepositions correctly.

> **Die Kinder sind im Bett.** (*The children are in bed.*) The preposition **in** (here it means *in*) uses dative case here to express location.

> **Die Kinder gehen ins Bett.** (*The children are going to bed.*) The preposition **in** (here it means *into*) uses accusative case to express movement.

> **Ich wohne über einer Buchhandlung.** (*I live above a bookstore.*) The preposition **über** (*over*) describes where it is, hence it is in dative case.

> **Der Zeppelin fliegt über die Stadt.** (*The zeppelin [blimp] is flying over the city.*) The preposition **über** (*over*) describes movement, so it uses the accusative.

Mastering preposition combinations

German has several quirky yet important prepositional phrases that you encounter on a regular basis. Try to remember these examples as complete phrases so you can use them later. To understand what sets these prepositional phrases apart from others, look at the following examples:

✔ **Zu Hause** and **nach Hause** are two prepositional phrases that are often confused. **Zu Hause** means *at home*. It indicates location. **Nach Hause** means *going home*. It implies movement, motion in the direction of home.

> **Wo ist Birgit? Sie ist zu Hause.** (*Where's Birgit? She's at home.*)

> **Wohin geht Lars? Er geht nach Hause.** (*Where is Lars going? He's going home.*)

✔ **Bis** (*till, until*) is an accusative preposition. What makes it different is the fact that it's used most often in combination with other prepositions, not as a standalone. Look at the following expressions:

> **Von 8.30 Uhr bis 19.00 Uhr** (*from 8:30 a.m. till 7 p.m.*).

> **Bis zum bitteren Ende** (*until the bitter end*); **zu** takes dative case: **zu + dem = zum.**

> **Bis ins kleinste Detail** (*in[to] the smallest detail*); **ins = in + das,** the accusative case.

> **Bis in den Abend hinein** (*on into the evening*); the phrase is in accusative case.

✔ **Entlang** (*along, down*) is the preposition that actually has three case combinations: accusative, dative, and genitive. In addition, **entlang** often follows the information it modifies. (It also functions as an adverb!) Look at the three examples of **entlang,** using the three cases:

> **Gehen Sie den Weg entlang.** (*Walk along the path.*) **Den Weg** is accusative case.

> **Die Grenze verläuft entlang dem Fluß.** (*The border follows the river.*) **Dem Fluß** is dative case.

> **Entlang des Ufers gibt es viele Schwäne.** (*There are a lot of swans along the shore.*) **Des Ufers** is genitive case. Usage of **entlang** in genitive case is typical in southern Germany and Austria.

✔ **Gegenüber** (*across from, opposite*), a true multitasker, is not only a dative preposition but also an adjective, adverb, and even a noun. As a preposition, it can be in front of or after its object; it makes no difference in meaning.

> **Wir wohnen gegenüber dem Park.** (*We live across from a park.*) The object, **dem Park,** follows **gegenüber.**

> **Der Präsident stand mir gegenüber.** (*The president was standing opposite me.*) The object, **mir,** precedes **gegenüber.** Technically speaking, prepositions that combine with verbs belong in a separate group called *prefix verbs.* (See Chapter 3 for the scoop on separable- and inseparable-prefix verbs.)

Chapter 6

Asking and Answering Questions

In This Chapter

▶ Giving or receiving a "yes" or "no"

▶ Obtaining and sharing information

*A*sking questions puts you in the conversational driver's seat. You use questions to initiate dialogues, get information, and clarify something you're not sure about. This chapter gets you up-to-speed on how to ask (and answer) different types of questions.

Formulating Yes/No Questions

German word order is easy to follow when you form a question that merits a yes or no answer. You simply flip the subject and the conjugated (main) verb: The verb is in first place, and the subject is in second place (where the verb usually goes in statements). Take a look at these examples in German and their English translations:

> **Leben Sie in einer Großstadt?** (*Do you live in a large city?*)

> **Bleibt sie hier?** (*Is she staying here?*)

> **Ist es kalt bei Ihnen im Winter?** (*Is it cold where you live in the winter?*)

Another type of question that elicits a yes or no response is the *tag question*. A tag question is simply what you tack onto the end of a statement to make it into a question. For example, you may say something like this, expecting the listener to agree with you: *The mall opens at 10, doesn't it?*

In English, the tag in a tag question depends on the subject and verb in the statement. The possibilities are practically endless in English: *isn't she?, do you?, can't we?, were you?, wouldn't it?,* and so on. The German equivalent is far simpler.

To form a tag question in German, just add **nicht?** (literally: *not?*) or **nicht wahr?** (literally: *not true?*) to the end of the sentence. If you want to elicit a response from someone as a means of checking your information, you can use **nicht** or **nicht wahr,** even if you're talking about something in the past, present, or future.

> **Sie fahren morgen nach Düsseldorf, nicht wahr?** (*You're going/driving to Düsseldorf tomorrow, aren't you?*)

> **Der Film war nicht besonders gut, nicht?** (*The movie wasn't especially good, was it?*)

Responding to a Yes/No Question

In general, saying "yes" or "no" in German is pretty easy; you simply answer **ja** or **nein.** But sometimes you need to express yourself with a range of positive or negative responses. The following sections give you the lowdown on how to properly say "yes" or "no" in any situation.

The affirmative way

When you want to show someone that you understand, that you're listening, and so on, you use **ja** (*yes*) and its extended family (for example, **Ja, das ist richtig** [*Yes, that's right*]). Use **ja** the way you do in English: to answer a question in the affirmative or to say that you agree to something. It can stand alone, or if **ja** is in a sentence, it generally comes at the beginning of an affirmative sentence, just as it does in English. In these instances, all you need to do is add **ja** to what you want to say.

When you get bored with saying **ja,** try a few variations that render the same meaning with a slightly different emphasis.

Table 6-1 contains nine alternatives for good ol' **ja.** The example sentences put these common substitutes into a context, and the English explanations describe the implications behind each expression.

Table 6-1	Alternatives for Ja		
Ja Equivalent	*Explanation*	*Example Sentence*	*Translation*
genau	*exactly, precisely* — the English translation sounds stilted, but not so to the German ear	**Genau, mein Familienname ist Schranner.**	*Exactly, my family name is Schranner.*
gewiss	*of course, sure enough* — somewhat formal-sounding in German	**Gewiss. Sie werden um 7.00 Uhr geweckt.**	*Of course. You'll be woken up at 7 a.m.*
ja, ja	*yes, yes* — can express enthusiasm or skepticism	**Ja, ja, das weiß ich schon.**	*Yes, yes, I already know that.*
jawohl	*exactly* — has a somewhat formal ring	**Jawohl, meine Frau kommt aus Sydney.**	*Exactly, my wife is from Sydney.*
klar	*of course* (literally: *clear* or *clearly*) — somewhat casual, colloquial tone	**Klar kann ich segeln.**	*Of course I know how to sail.*
natürlich	*naturally* — neutral, neither formal nor colloquial	**Natürlich helfen wir Ihnen.**	*Naturally, we'll help you.*
richtig	*right* — neutral, neither formal nor colloquial	**Richtig. Er mietet ein Auto.**	*Right. He's renting a car.*
selbstverständlich	*certainly* — good choice for business, formal situations	**Selbstverständlich lade ich Sie zum Mittagessen ein.**	*Certainly, I'm inviting you to lunch.*
sicher	*certainly, sure*	**Sicher mache ich das Licht aus.**	*Sure, I'll turn off the light.*

Notice that in the example sentences, when the **ja** substitute is followed by a comma or a period, you start the next phrase in the usual German word order of subject followed by the verb in second position. (In the example sentences, the comma and period are interchangeable.) When the **ja** replacement word functions as the first element in the sentence (no comma or period), the verb follows in second position.

When you want to add more emphasis to show that you *really* understand or agree with someone, you can add **ja** or **aber** (*but*) to the expressions in Table 6-1. Take a look:

> **Ja, klar!** (*Yes, of course!*)
>
> **Aber natürlich!** (*Certainly!*)
>
> **Aber selbstverständlich!** (*Why, certainly!*)
>
> **Ja, sicher!** (*Yes, sure!*)

The preceding examples place the **ja** words at the beginning of the sentence. However, when you want to express understanding or agreement within a sentence, you can construct sentences that use these words in more or less fixed expressions, such as **genau richtig** or **es ist (mir) klar.** In addition, **genau, gewiss, klar, natürlich, richtig, selbstverständlich,** and **sicher** can work as adjectives or in some cases as adverbs, and they have similar meanings. (See Chapter 5 for more on adjectives.)

> **Das wird selbstverständlich gemacht.** (*That will certainly be done.*)
>
> **Es ist mir klar, dass ich abnehmen soll.** (*I realize that I should lose weight.* Literally: *It's clear to me that I should lose weight.*)
>
> **Die Straßen waren gewiss sehr gefährlich nach dem Sturm.** (*The streets were certainly very dangerous after the storm.*)
>
> **Sie haben es genau richtig geraten.** (*You guessed it exactly right.*)

The negative way

Saying "no" in German is plain and simple: **nein.** However, when you want to negate an action, or an object or person, you have two ways to express *not* (or *not any*): **kein** and **nicht.** Getting these two expressions straight is a matter of knowing what they negate in a sentence.

The next sections help you figure out when to use **kein** and when to use **nicht.** They also reveal how to say "no" politely (because a straightforward **nein** can come off as rude).

Negating with kein

Kein (*no, not, not any*) functions as an adjective; it describes nouns by expressing negation. Here are some examples: **kein Polizist** (*no policeman*), **keine Jeans** (*no jeans*), **kein Brot** (*no bread*).

Before you can jump in and start adding **kein** into your sentences, you need to know the gender and case of the noun you're negating. Look at the following sentence: **Kein Polizist hat einen leichten Job** (*no policeman has an easy job*). **Kein Polizist** is the subject of the sentence, so it's in nominative case.

Table 6-2 shows how to remember the endings for **kein,** with the case and gender endings in bold. Masculine and neuter are grouped together, and feminine and plural are in one column. (*Note:* This table is also valid for all the **ein-** words except for **ein** itself, which has no plural form.)

Table 6-2	Endings of Kein	
Case	*Masculine / Neuter*	*Feminine / Plural*
Nominative	kein	kein**e**
Accusative	kein**en** (masc.), kein (n.)	kein**e**
Dative	kein**em**	kein**er** (fem.), kein**en** (pl.)
Genitive	kein**es**	kein**er**

Notice that the masculine and neuter endings are almost all the same for **kein;** the accusative case is the only one that differs. You can also remember feminine and plural together, keeping in mind that the dative case is the only one that isn't the same for the two genders. Look at these example sentences with **kein** in the four cases, followed by the English equivalent and the grammar note explaining the gender:

✔ Nominative case: **Keine Menschen leben auf der Insel.** (*No people live on the island.*) **Menschen** (plural) is the subject of the sentence, so **keine Menschen** is nominative plural.

✔ Accusative case: **Nach dem grossen Abendessen hatte ich keinen Hunger.** (*I wasn't hungry after the big dinner.*) Literally, **ich hatte keinen Hunger** means *I had no hunger.* **Der Hunger** (masculine) changes to the accusative singular **keinen Hunger** because it's the object of the sentence.

✔ Dative case: **In keinem alten Auto gibt es GPS.** (*There's no GPS in any old car[s].*) Literally, **in keinem alten Auto gibt es GPS** means *in no old car is there GPS.* The prepositional phrase **in keinem alten Auto** is in dative case; therefore, **das Auto** becomes **keinem (alten) Auto.**

✔ Genitive case: **Während keiner Nacht in der letzten Woche habe ich gut geschlafen.** (*I didn't sleep well [during] any night last week.*) Literally, **während keiner Nacht in der letzten Woche habe ich gut geschlafen** means *during no night in the past week did I sleep well.* **Während** (*during*) is a genitive preposition, and **die Nacht** is feminine singular. You need the genitive case ending **-er** for **kein.**

Negating with nicht

The nuts and bolts of **nicht** are straightforward as far as its form is concerned. **Nicht** is all you need to know (unlike **kein,** which has case and gender endings, as explained in the preceding section). **Nicht** generally negates a verb: **nicht einladen** (*not to invite*), **nicht fahren** (*not to drive, travel*), **nicht feiern** (*not to celebrate*). But it can also negate an adjective, as in **nicht interessant** (*not interesting*), or an adverb, as in **nicht pünktlich** (*not on time*).

What you do need to figure out is how to position **nicht** in a sentence. Because **nicht** is an adverb, it negates the action of the verb or modifies an adjective or an adverb, and it's generally next to these parts of speech. For example:

Sie fliegen nicht nach London. (*They're not flying to London.*) **Nicht** directly follows the verb in this sentence, negating the idea that they're flying.

Martin spricht nicht gut Deutsch. (*Martin doesn't speak good German.*) In this sentence, **nicht** tells you that Martin's ability to speak German is not good, so **nicht** immediately follows the verb.

Gestern kamen wir nicht pünktlich zum Termin. (*Yesterday we didn't get to our appointment on time.*) **Nicht** links with the adverb **pünktlich** (*on time*), and you place it before **pünktlich.**

Das Buch ist nicht interessant. (*The book isn't interesting.*) The negation connects the verb **ist** (*is*) and the adjective **interessant** (*interesting*); **nicht** modifies **interessant**, so you place it in front of the adjective.

Placement is the more complex part of **nicht,** so Table 6-3 explains some of the guidelines. Most of the time, though, if you don't place **nicht** perfectly, you'll still be understandable in spoken or written German.

Table 6-3   Guidelines for Positioning Nicht

Position of Nicht	Example Sentence	Translation
Follows		
A conjugated verb	Maria fährt **nicht** nach Kiel.	*Maria isn't driving to Kiel.*
A conjugated verb and precedes a separable prefix	Felix und Gretl sehen **nicht** fern. (**Fernsehen** is a separable prefix verb.)	*Felix and Gretl aren't watching TV.*
Most specific adverbs of time	Ich war gestern **nicht** zu Hause. (**Gestern** is the specific adverb of time.)	*I wasn't at home yesterday.*
Comes at the end of		
Yes/no questions	Essen Sie den Apfel **nicht?**	*Aren't you going to eat the apple?*
A sentence or question with a direct object	Ich kenne diesen Mann **nicht.** (**Diesen Mann** is the direct object.)	*I don't know that man.*

(continued)

Table 6-3 *(continued)*

Position of Nicht	Example Sentence	Translation
Precedes		
Most adjectives	Das Hotel ist **nicht** gemütlich.	*The hotel isn't cozy.* (**Gemütlich** is the adjective.)
Most adverbs, except for specific adverbs of time	Ihr lauft **nicht** schnell. (**Schnell** is the adverb.)	*You don't run fast.*
Infinitives connected to a verb	Ich gehe **nicht** einkaufen. (**Einkaufen** is the infinitive.)	*I'm not going shopping.*
Most prepositional phrases	Dieser Käse kommt **nicht** aus Frankreich. (**Aus Frankreich** is the prepositional phrase.)	*This cheese isn't from France.*
The combinations of parts in a sentence (usually)	Matthias geht **nicht** sehr oft in die Bibliothek. (Two parts are here — **sehr oft** and **in die Bibliothek.**)	*Matthias doesn't go to the library very often.*

Avoiding blunt negative answers

You don't want to sound overly negative when answering yes/no-type questions with a straight **nein** because otherwise the listener may be put off. You can politely answer some questions negatively by adding a few words to cushion the impact.

How can you avoid being blunt in polite conversation? You can make a positive impression on German speakers when giving negative replies by using *idiomatic expressions* — fixed phrases — that help you avoid sounding overly negative. Consider this exchange:

> **Haben Sie Kleingeld für 10€?** (*Do you have change for 10€?*)

> **Nein, es tut mir leid.** (*No, I'm sorry. I don't.*) Adding **es tut mir leid** softens the straight **nein** response.

Table 6-4 provides a sampling of expressions that help you avoid sounding too strongly negative.

Table 6-4	Avoiding Bluntness with Negative Answers	
Phrase	*English Equivalent*	*Comments*
Es tut mir leid	*I'm sorry*	The apology **Es tut mir leid** prefaces the rest of the information.
fast keine (Zeit)	*hardly any (time)*	**Fast keine Zeit** (*hardly any time*) is the same as **kaum Zeit.**
praktisch kein	*practically no*	You can also use **praktisch** in the positive sense: Sie ist **praktisch** fertig. (*She's practically/virtually ready.*)
Im Grunde genommen	*basically*	The signal of a refusal — **Im Grunde genommen** — comes at the beginning of the sentence, softening the negative.
nicht hundert-prozentig/nicht ganz	*not 100%/not completely*	You don't need to admit that you understand only 70%. Chances are, the speaker will repeat him/herself. Stating **nein** flatly may not get you anywhere.
nicht nur (. . . sondern auch)	*not only (. . . but also)*	**nicht nur** (*not only*) can be linked like this: **Nicht nur** mein Vater, **sondern auch** mein Großvater kam aus Irland. (*Not only my father but also my grandfather came from Ireland.*)
Ich habe nicht die leiseste Ahnung	*I haven't the faintest idea*	This expression is fixed and can also be stated like this: Ich **habe keine Ahnung.** (*I have no idea.*)

Asking Informational Questions

Sometimes a simple "yes" or "no" doesn't cut it and you need more information in response to your question. The following sections show you what to say when you want to get more detailed answers.

Using question words

You need question words such as *who, what, where,* and *when* to gather specific information, but you can also use a young kid's tactic of asking **wer** (*who*), **was** (*what*), **warum** (*why*), and so on as a tool for engaging people in conversation. Doing so is a useful tactic because it gives you more control over the direction of the discussion.

The inverted word order for yes/no questions (see the earlier section "Formulating Yes/No Questions") is the same for information-gathering questions, only the question word (or phrase) comes first. Thus, the word order for info-gathering questions is question word + verb + subject, such as **Warum ist der Himmel blau?** (*Why is the sky blue?*) or **Wann fahren wir nach Hause?** (*When are we driving home?*).

Table 6-5 lists 12 German question words and phrases with their English equivalents and an example question in German with its English translation.

Table 6-5   Question Words and Example Questions

Question Word or Phrase	Example Sentence	Translation
wie (*how*)	**Wie heißen Sie?**	*What is your name?*
wie viele (*how many*)	**Wie viele Personen arbeiten in Ihrer Firma?**	*How many people work in your company?*
wie viel (*how much*)	**Wie viel kostet die Karte?**	*How much is the ticket?*
was (*what*)	**Was machen wir nach der Pause?**	*What are we doing after the break?*
was für (*what kind of*)	**Was für ein Auto fahren Sie?**	*What kind of car do you drive?*
wann (*when*)	**Wann beginnt das Konzert?**	*When does the concert begin?*
wo (*where*)	**Wo wohnen Sie?**	*Where do you live?*
woher (*where . . . from*)	**Woher kommen Sie?**	*Where are you from?*

Question Word or Phrase	Example Sentence	Translation
wohin (*where . . . [to]*)	**Wohin fährt der Bus?**	*Where does the bus go (to)?*
welcher/welche/ welches (*which*)	**Welche Straßenbahn soll ich nehmen? (die Straßenbahn)**	*Which tram should I take?*
wer (nominative) (*who*), **wen** (accusative) (*whom, who*), **wem** (dative) (*who*), **wessen** (genitive) (*whose*)	**Wer ist Ihr Chef?**	*Who is your boss?*
warum (*why*)	**Warum hält der Zug jetzt (an)?**	*Why is the train stopping now?*

Calling the case in question

The question words **welch-** and **wer** are interrogative pronouns. You need to be aware of the role that case and noun gender play in making questions with these words.

Welcher/welche/welches (*which*) is an interrogative pronoun with three versions to correspond with the three noun genders **der/die/das: welcher Computer** (*which computer*), **welche Frau** (*which woman*), **welches Auto** (*which car*). You need to remember that it has adjective endings — in other words, the case endings of the noun it's describing. For example, consider **Mit welchem Bus soll ich fahren?** (*Which bus should I take? Literally: With which bus should I drive/travel?*). The preposition **mit** uses the dative case, and **der Bus** is masculine, so **mit welchem Bus** uses the masculine dative singular form of **welch-** in the prepositional phrase.

Wer (*who*) is an interrogative pronoun that has three other forms. **Wer** is the nominative case, **wen** (*whom, who*) is accusative, **wem** (*who*) is dative, and **wessen** (*whose*) is genitive.

The question phrase **was für** (*what kind of*) contains the accusative preposition **für**, but the preposition **für** in **was für** doesn't determine the case; rather, the other information in the question does. Look at the following questions:

- ✔ **Was für ein Fahrschein ist das?** (*What kind of ticket is that?*) The subject is **Fahrschein,** which is a masculine gender noun. **Ein Fahrschein** is in the nominative case; it's the subject of the question.

- ✔ **Was für einen Fahrschein brauche ich?** (*What kind of ticket do I need?*) **Fahrschein** is a masculine gender noun. **Einen Fahrschein** is in the accusative case; it's the direct object of the question.

Formulating compound question words with wo-

Adding the question word **wo-** (*where*) in front of a preposition results in a compound question word. The **wo-** signals to the listener that a question is coming up and that it's going to be about the object of the preposition. The listener, therefore, gets the most important information first in the question.

The German word order in questions beginning with **wo-** compounds such as **worüber** (*what about, what over*) may seem odd at first: **Worüber spricht sie?** (*What's she talking about?* Literally: *What over [about] is she talking?*) However, it's standard fare in German.

A second important function of the compound question words using **wo-** is to prompt the listener that the question you're asking allows an open-ended answer: **Wofür sind Sie?** (*What are you for?*) The listener may answer like this: **Ich bin für den Frieden** (*I'm for peace*) or **Ich bin für einen Spaziergang im Park** (*I'm [up] for a walk in the park*).

The meaning of the preposition in the compound with **wo-** may be different from the original meaning.

Table 6-6 shows the most common compounds formed by adding **wo-** to the prepositions. When the preposition begins with a vowel, the letter **r** is inserted between the two elements of the question word (for example, **wo + r + in = worin**).

Table 6-6	Questioning Using Wo- Compounds	
German Preposition	**Translation**	**Wo- Compound**
an	*on, at, to*	**woran**
auf	*on top of, to*	**worauf**
aus	*out of, from*	**woraus**
durch	*through, by*	**wodurch**
für	*for*	**wofür**
gegen	*against*	**wogegen**
in	*in, inside of*	**worin**
hinter	*behind, after*	**wohinter**
mit	*with, by*	**womit**
nach	*after, to*	**wonach**
über	*over, above*	**worüber**
um	*around*	**worum**
unter	*under*	**worunter**
von	*from, by*	**wovon**
vor	*in front of, before*	**wovor**
zu	*to, at*	**wozu**

Providing Information

This section is chock-full of tips on how to answer questions that ask you for information in German.

✔ When you see or hear a question with **warum?** (*why?*), you answer with **weil** (*because*) or simply give the explanation that's requested.

- **Warum machst du das Fenster zu?** (*Why are you closing the window?*)

  Weil es zieht. (*Because there's a draft.*)

  Mir ist kalt. (*I'm cold.*)

✔ When you see or hear a question with **woher?** (*where . . . from?*), you tell where someone or something is from, and use **aus** (*from*) in your response before stating the place where someone or something is from.

- **Woher kommen Sie?** (*Where are you from?*)

  Wir kommen aus Boston. (*We're from Boston.*)

✔ When you see or hear a question with **wohin?** (*where . . . to?*), you answer with the information that's requested and use **nach** (*to*) in your response before naming the place where someone or something is going to.

- **Wohin fährt der Zug?** (*Where's the train going [to]?*)

  Er fährt nach Grassau. (*It's going to Grassau.*)

✔ When you see or hear a question beginning with **Um wie viel Uhr?** (*At what time?*), you answer with the time, and you use **um** (*at*) before the time expression.

- **Um wie viel Uhr beginnt das Konzert?** (*What time does the concert begin?*)

  Es beginnt um 19.30. (*It begins at 7:30 p.m.*)

✔ When you see or hear a question with **wann?** (*At what time?*), you answer with a specific time or a general time.

- **Wann gehen wir ins Kino?** (*When are we going to the cinema?*)

  Um 21.00. (*At 9 p.m.*) (specific time)

  Am Samstag. (*On Saturday.*) (general time)

✔ If you see or hear a question that contains **wie?** (*how?*), you answer by describing something or someone. **Wie** also appears in several fixed expressions.

- **Wie war der Flug?** (*How was the flight?*)

  Zu lang. (*Too long.*)

Following are some frequently used expressions with **wie:**

- **Wie sagt man** "headache" **auf Deutsch?** (*How do you say "headache" in German?*)

  Kopfweh. (*Headache.*)

- **Wie ist Ihre Adresse?** (*What is your address?*)

Landsbergerstraße 358, 80337 München.
(*Landsberger Street 358, 80337 Munich.*)

- **Wie heißen Sie?** (*What's your name?*)

  Kellsey Dodd. (*Kellsey Dodd.*)

- **Wie geht's?** (*How are you?/How's it going?*)
  (informal)

  Nicht schlecht. (*Not bad.*)

- **Wie geht es Ihnen?** (*How are you?*) (formal)

  Sehr gut, danke. (*Very well, thank you.*)

Chapter 7

Stepping Back in the Past

· ·

In This Chapter

▶ Understanding the present perfect

▶ Getting to know the simple past

· ·

*G*erman speakers have two ways of describing past events: the present perfect tense and the simple past tense. Simply put, the present perfect is common in the spoken language, whereas the simple past is considered the narrative past (so you come across it more frequently in written German). I show you how to form and use both past tenses in this chapter.

Conversing with Present Perfect

Germans use the present perfect tense to talk about past activities. This tense is commonly described as the *conversational past* because — naturally — you use it in conversation.

The present perfect in German has two elements:

- ✔ An *auxiliary verb,* also known as a *helping verb* (most German verbs use **haben,** although some use **sein;** English present perfect uses *have*)

- ✔ A past participle (examples are **gegangen** [*gone*], **gearbeitet** [*worked*], and **getrunken** [*drunk*])

The majority of verbs form the present perfect with the auxiliary verb **haben** (*to have*) plus the past participle of the verb you want to use. The two main categories of verbs, which are classified by the way the past participle is formed, are called *weak* and *strong* verbs.

Although using **haben** is most common, some verbs may use a form of **sein** as the auxiliary verb. See the section "Forming present perfect with the auxiliary verb **sein**" for details.

To conjugate a verb in the present perfect with **haben,** you choose the simple present-tense form of **haben: ich habe, du hast, er/sie/es hat, wir haben, ihr habt, sie haben,** or **Sie haben.** You then add the past participle of the verb.

German has only the one verb tense, the present perfect, to represent three tenses in English. Here are three acceptable translations of **Sie haben in Wien gelebt:**

- ✔ **Present perfect:** *They have lived in Vienna* (expresses that they may still live there).

- ✔ **Simple past:** *They lived in Vienna* (says they no longer live there).

- ✔ **Past continuous:** *They were living in Vienna* (talks about a relationship between two completed past actions — the other past action may be described in a previous or subsequent sentence or in the same sentence).

The differences in the present perfect come about when you want to add a time element, such as **gestern** (*yesterday*): **Gestern habe ich einen Kojoten gesehen** (*Yesterday, I saw a coyote*). You use the present perfect in German, but in English, you use *saw* (the simple past).

Forming present perfect with weak verbs

Two types of weak verbs exist in German: regular and irregular. You need to know how to form the present perfect with both of them if you want to speak accurately about the past.

Regular weak verbs

Regular weak verbs are the largest group of verbs. To form the past participle, take the unchanged present-tense stem and add the **ge-** prefix and the ending **-t** or **-et.** You need the **-et** ending in the following cases:

✔ For verbs whose stem ends in **-d** or **-t** (for example, **heiraten** [*to marry*] becomes **geheiratet** [*married*])

✔ For some verbs whose stem ends in **-m** or **-n** (**regnen** [*to rain*] becomes **geregnet** [*rained*])

✔ For verbs recently taken from English (such as **flirten** [*to flirt*] changes to **geflirtet** [*flirted*])

The following table shows the present perfect conjugation of the regular weak verb **arbeiten** (*to work*). To do this, you conjugate **haben** in the appropriate person and then add the past participle. To create the past participle, you chop off the ending **-en,** take the stem **arbeit,** and add **ge-** and **-et** like this: **ge- + arbeit + -et = gearbeitet.**

arbeiten (*to work*)	
ich **habe gearbeitet**	wir **haben gearbeitet**
du **hast gearbeitet**	ihr **habt gearbeitet**
er/sie/es **hat gearbeitet**	sie **haben gearbeitet**
Sie **haben gearbeitet**	
Sie **hat** im Herbst bei der Filmgesellschaft **gearbeitet.** (*She worked at the film company in the fall.*)	

Table 7-1 shows some regular weak verbs with their past participles.

Table 7-1	Past Participles of Regular Weak Verbs		
Infinitive	*Past Participle*	*Infinitive*	*Past Participle*
arbeiten (*to work*)	**gearbeitet** (*worked*)	**lieben** (*to love*)	**geliebt** (*loved*)
drucken (*to print*)	**gedruckt** (*printed*)	**lernen** (*to learn*)	**gelernt** (*learned*)
führen (*to lead*)	**geführt** (*led*)	**machen** (*to make*)	**gemacht** (*made*)
hören (*to hear*)	**gehört** (*heard*)	**passen** (*to fit*)	**gepasst** (*fit*)
hoffen (*to hope*)	**gehofft** (*hoped*)	**regnen** (*to rain*)	**geregnet** (*rained*)

(continued)

Table 7-1 *(continued)*

Infinitive	Past Participle	Infinitive	Past Participle
kaufen (*to buy*)	gekauft (*bought*)	sagen (*to say*)	gesagt (*said*)
kosten (*to cost*)	gekostet (*cost*)	schenken (*to give[a present]*)	geschenkt (*given*)
kriegen (*to get*)	gekriegt (*gotten/got*)	spielen (*to play*)	gespielt (*played*)
lächeln (*to smile*)	gelächelt (*smiled*)	surfen (*to surf*)	gesurft (*surfed*)
leben (*to live*)	gelebt (*lived*)	tanzen (*to dance*)	getanzt (*danced*)

Irregular weak verbs

Very few weak verbs are irregular, meaning they have the prefix **ge-** and the ending **-t,** but they don't follow the same pattern as the regular weak verbs. The present-tense stem changes when you put it in the past participle.

To form irregular weak verbs in the present perfect, conjugate **haben** in the present tense and then add the past participle. Check out the following example with the verb **denken** (*to think*).

denken (*to think*)	
ich **habe gedacht**	wir **haben gedacht**
du **hast gedacht**	ihr **habt gedacht**
er/sie/es **hat gedacht**	sie **haben gedacht**
Sie **haben gedacht**	
Luka **hat** oft an seine Frau **gedacht.** (*Luka often thought about his wife.*)	

Table 7-2 lists the irregular weak verbs with their past participles.

Table 7-2   Past Participles of Irregular Weak Verbs

Infinitive	Past Participle
brennen (*to burn*)	**gebrannt** (*burned*)
bringen (*to bring*)	**gebracht** (*brought*)
denken (*to think*)	**gedacht** (*thought*)
kennen (*to know a person*)	**gekannt** (*known a person*)
nennen (*to name, call*)	**genannt** (*named, called*)
wissen (*to know information*)	**gewusst** (*known information*)

Forming present perfect with strong verbs

Identifying a *strong verb* is fairly easy. Its past participle ends in **-en**. (The one exception is the verb **tun** [*to do*]; its past participle is **getan** [*done*].) In most strong verbs, the past participle begins with **ge-**.

To form the present perfect with strong verbs, you conjugate **haben** in the appropriate person and then add the past participle. Following is an example using the verb **trinken** (*to drink*).

trinken (*to drink*)	
ich **habe getrunken**	wir **haben getrunken**
du **hast getrunken**	ihr **habt getrunken**
er/sie/es **hat getrunken**	sie **haben getrunken**
Sie **haben getrunken**	
Wir **haben** gestern viel Mineralwasser **getrunken**. (*We drank a lot of mineral water yesterday.*)	

Table 7-3 shows some other strong verbs with their past participles.

Table 7-3	Past Participles of Strong Verbs		
Infinitive	*Past Participle*	*Infinitive*	*Past Participle*
backen (*to bake*)	**gebacken** (*baked*)	**schreiben** (*to write*)	**geschrieben** (*written*)
beginnen (*to begin*)	**begonnen** (*begun*)	**singen** (*to sing*)	**gesungen** (*sung*)
essen (*to eat*)	**gegessen** (*eaten*)	**sitzen** (*to sit*)	**gesessen** (*sat*)
finden (*to find*)	**gefunden** (*found*)	**sprechen** (*to speak, talk*)	**gesprochen** (*spoken, talked*)
geben (*to give*)	**gegeben** (*given*)	**stehen** (*to stand*)	**gestanden** (*stood*)
halten (*to hold*)	**gehalten** (*held*)	**tragen** (*to wear*)	**getragen** (*worn*)
heißen (*to be called*)	**geheißen** (*been called*)	**treffen** (*to meet*)	**getroffen** (*met*)
helfen (*to help*)	**geholfen** (*helped*)	**trinken** (*to drink*)	**getrunken** (*drunk*)
lassen (to leave, let)	**gelassen** (*left, let*)	**tun** (*to do*)	**getan** (*done*)
lesen (*to read*)	**gelesen** (*read*)	**verlassen** (*to leave*)	**verlassen** (*left*)
liegen (*to lie, be located*)	**gelegen** (*lain, been located*)	**verlieren** (*to lose*)	**verloren** (*lost*)
nehmen (*to take*)	**genommen** (*taken*)	**verstehen** (*to understand*)	**verstanden** (*understood*)
rufen (*to call*)	**gerufen** (*called*)	**waschen** (*to wash*)	**gewaschen** (*washed*)
schlafen (*to sleep*)	**geschlafen** (*slept*)	**ziehen** (*to pull*)	**gezogen** (*pulled*)

Forming present perfect with the auxiliary verb sein

Although the majority of verbs formed in the present perfect use a form of **haben,** some verbs form the present perfect with the auxiliary verb **sein** (*to be*) plus the past participle of the verb you want to use. All these verbs that use **sein** share these similarities:

✔ They indicate some form of motion.

✔ They show a change in some condition — as with **werden** (*to become*) — or some motion to or from a place, such as **kommen** (*to come*).

✔ They don't have a direct object, which means they're *intransitive*. For example, the verb **laufen** (*to run*) is intransitive: **Wir sind schnell gelaufen.** (*We ran fast.*) An example of a transitive verb (with a direct object) is **trinken** (*to drink*), and it looks like this: **Ich habe eine Tasse Tee getrunken.** (*I drank a cup of tea.*)

Generally, you form the past participle with **ge-** + the stem from the infinitive + the ending **-en:** For example, **kommen** (*to come*) becomes **gekommen** (come). However, you also have the types of past participles that have gone through some spelling changes from the original infinitive form: **Gehen** (*to go, walk*) changes to **gegangen** (*gone, walked*).

To form the present perfect with **sein,** you first conjugate the present tense of the verb **sein** and then add the right past participle. Look at the following example with **fahren** (*to drive*).

fahren (*to drive*)	
ich **bin gefahren**	wir **sind gefahren**
du **bist gefahren**	ihr **seid gefahren**
er/sie/es **ist gefahren**	sie **sind gefahren**
Sie **sind gefahren**	
Bist du die ganze Nacht **gefahren?** (*Did you drive all night?*)	

Even in conversation, using the simple past of **sein** is a lot more common than using the present perfect; for example: **Wie war der Flug von Zürich nach San Francisco?** (*How was the flight from Zürich to San Francisco?*)

Look at Table 7-4, which shows a list of verbs that use **sein** in the present perfect. Some past participles have no stem change; others go through contortions to form the past participle.

Table 7-4	Verbs Conjugated with Sein in the Present Perfect		
Infinitive	*Sein + Past Participle*	*Infinitive*	*Sein + Past Participle*
bleiben (*to stay, remain*)	**ist geblieben** (*stayed, remained*)	**reiten** (*to ride [horseback]*)	**ist geritten** (*ridden*)
fahren (*to drive*)	**ist gefahren** (*driven*)	**schwimmen** (*to swim*)	**ist geschwommen** (*swum*)
fallen (*to fall*)	**ist gefallen** (*fallen*)	**sein** (*to be*)	**ist gewesen** (*been*)
fliegen (*to fly*)	**ist geflogen** (*flown*)	**steigen** (*to climb*)	**ist gestiegen** (*climbed*)
fließen (*to flow, run*)	**ist geflossen** (*flowed, run*)	**sterben** (*to die*)	**ist gestorben** (*died*)
gehen (*to go, walk*)	**ist gegangen** (*gone, walked*)	**wachsen** (*to grow*)	**ist gewachsen** (*grown*)
kommen (*to come*)	**ist gekommen** (*come*)	**werden** (*to become*)	**ist geworden** (*become*)
laufen (*to run, walk*)	**ist gelaufen** (*run, walked*)		

Forming present perfect with oddball verbs

You need to do a bit of juggling with some groups of German verbs when you form the present perfect. One group is known as the **separable-prefix verbs.** They're recognizable by a prefix, such as **auf-,** that separates from the main verb in some verb tenses. Another group is called the **inseparable-prefix verbs:** They're identified by a prefix, such as **be-,** that doesn't separate from a main verb. A third group consists of verbs ending in **-ieren** in the infinitive form.

In the following sections, you figure out how to identify these verbs and form the present perfect with them.

Separating the separable-prefix verbs

With separable-prefix verbs, you leave the prefix at the front of the verb, squish **ge-** in the middle, and follow up with the rest of the participle. Most of the commonly used verbs in this group resemble strong verbs (which have a past participle ending in **-en,** as described in the earlier section "Forming present perfect with strong verbs.")

You put together the present perfect of separable-prefix verbs by conjugating **haben** or **sein** in the present tense and adding the past participle. So if the infinitive is **anrufen** (*to call [on the phone]*), you get the past participle **angerufen** (*called*), which has the three elements **an** + **ge** + **rufen.** Take a look at the conjugation of **fernsehen** (*to watch TV*).

fernsehen (*to watch TV*)	
ich **habe ferngesehen**	wir **haben ferngesehen**
du **hast ferngesehen**	ihr **habt ferngesehen**
er/sie/es **hat ferngesehen**	sie **haben ferngesehen**
Sie **haben ferngesehen**	
Habt ihr am Wochenende **ferngesehen?** (*Did you watch TV on the weekend?*)	

You pronounce the separable-prefix verbs with the stress on the first syllable, which is the prefix.

Table 7-5 shows you what the past participle looks like. Note that I've included **ist** before the past participles that need the infinitive **sein.**

Table 7-5   Verbs with Separable Prefixes

Infinitive	Past Participle	Infinitive	Past Participle
anfangen (*to begin, start*)	**angefangen** (*begun, started*)	**mitbringen** (*to bring along*)	**mitgebracht** (*brought along*)
ankommen (*to arrive*)	**ist angekommen** (*arrived*)	**mitmachen** (*to join in*)	**mitgemacht** (*joined in*)
anrufen (*to call*)	**angerufen** (*called*)	**stattfinden** (*to take place*)	**stattgefunden** (*taken place*)
aufgeben (*to give up, check [luggage]*)	**aufgegeben** (*given up, checked [luggage]*)	**vorhaben** (*to plan*)	**vorgehabt** (*planned*)

(continued)

Table 7-5 *(continued)*

Infinitive	Past Participle	Infinitive	Past Participle
aussehen (*to look [like]*)	ausgesehen (*looked [like]*)	zurückgehen (*to decline, go back*)	ist zurückgegangen (*declined, gone back*)
einkaufen (*to go shopping*)	eingekauft (*gone shopping*)	zusammenfassen (*to summarize*)	zusammengefasst (*summarized*)
einladen (*to invite*)	eingeladen (*invited*)	zusammenkommen (*to meet*)	ist zusammengekommen (*met*)
fernsehen (*to watch TV*)	ferngesehen (*watched TV*)		

Sticking together with inseparable-prefix verbs

With inseparable-prefix verbs, the past participle can have a strong verb ending (**-en**) or a weak verb ending (**-t** or **-et**), but the rest is relatively easy. To help you distinguish them from their separable-prefix counterparts, just keep these three characteristics of inseparable-prefix verbs in mind:

 ✓ The prefix always sticks to the rest of the verb, including the past participle (hence the inseparable part of the name).

 ✓ You don't add the prefix **ge-** to the past participle.

 ✓ You don't stress the prefix. Look at the infinitive **erken'nen** (*to recognize*) and its past participle **erkannt'** (*recognized*).

You put together the present perfect of inseparable-prefix verbs by conjugating **haben** in the present tense and adding the past participle. Check out the conjugation of **bekommen** (*to get, receive*).

bekommen (*to get, receive*)	
ich **habe bekommen**	wir **haben bekommen**
du **hast bekommen**	ihr **habt bekommen**
er/sie/es **hat bekommen**	sie **haben bekommen**
Sie **haben bekommen**	
Warum **hast** du die Zeitung heute nicht **bekommen?** (*Why didn't you get the newspaper today?*)	

Table 7-6 is a list of some inseparable-prefix verbs with their past participles. Notice how similar the two forms of the verbs are — in fact, a few are exactly the same.

Table 7-6	Verbs with Inseparable Prefixes		
Infinitive	*Past Participle*	*Infinitive*	*Past Participle*
beantworten (*to answer*)	beantwortet (*answered*)	gebrauchen (*to use, make use of*)	gebraucht (*used, made use of*)
bekommen (*to get, receive*)	bekommen (*gotten, received*)	gefallen (*to like*)	gefallen (*liked*)
besuchen (*to visit*)	besucht (*visited*)	gehören (*to belong to*)	gehört (*belonged to*)
bezahlen (*to pay*)	bezahlt (*paid*)	gewinnen (*to win*)	gewonnen (*won*)
erkennen (*to recognize*)	erkannt (*recognized*)	missverstehen (*to misunderstand*)	missverstanden (*misunderstood*)
erklären (*to explain*)	erklärt (*explained*)	vergessen (*to forget*)	vergessen (*forgotten*)
erzählen (*to tell*)	erzählt (*told*)	verlieren (*to lose*)	verloren (*lost*)

Dealing with verbs ending in -ieren

The **-ieren** verbs are oddball verbs for several reasons. First, they end in **-ieren,** unlike mainstream verbs, which end in **-en.** Plus, they form the past participle without **ge-** but with **-t** at the end.

You can usually recognize the meanings of **-ieren** verbs, and the English equivalent of the infinitive often ends in *-ify* (**verifizieren** = *to verify*) or *-ate* (**vibrieren** = *to vibrate*).

When forming the present perfect with **-ieren** verbs, all you need to know is the following:

  ✔ You form the past participle without **ge-.**

  ✔ You always form the past participle with **-t.**

Look at how easily you can use these verbs:

  ✔ **fotografieren** (*to photograph*): **Der Journalist <u>hat</u> die Demonstration <u>fotografiert</u>.** (*The journalist photographed the demonstration.*)

✔ **dekorieren** (*to decorate*): **Vor dem Neujahrsfest <u>haben</u> wir das Wohnzimmer <u>dekoriert</u>.** (*Before the New Year's Eve party, we decorated the living room.*)

✔ **probieren** (*to try, sample*): **<u>Hast</u> du die Torte schon <u>probiert</u>? Sie ist lecker!** (*Have you tried the torte [cake] yet? It's delicious!*)

Writing with the Simple Past

In German, the verb tense of choice when narrating fact or fiction is the simple past tense — for example, **er ging** (*he went*), **wir mussten** (*we had to*), or **ich sprach** (*I spoke*).

The applications of the simple past are quite different when you compare German and English.

✔ German tends to use the simple past in written language, especially newspapers, books, written texts, narrated stories, and even fairy tales. English uses the simple past for spoken and written language.

✔ In German, the simple past is also a means of describing past events not connected to the present. English, on the other hand, uses the simple past to describe an action that's completed in the past, often with a reference to the past: *last month, in 2010,* or *when I was 23.*

The simple past verb form isn't too difficult to master. You just need to know that several types of endings exist according to which category the verb falls into:

✔ Regular verbs, also called *weak verbs*

✔ Irregular verbs, also known as *strong verbs*

✔ Other irregular verbs such as **sein, haben,** and the modal auxiliary verbs, also called *helping verbs*

Note: A fourth category of verbs, the separable-prefix verbs, includes verbs that have a prefix, such as **ab-,** or a preposition, such as **mit-,** in front of the verb; these verbs may be regular or irregular. The prefix is separated when you conjugate the verb, and it's generally placed at the end of the phrase. Two examples are **abfahren** (*to leave*) and **mitkommen** (*to come along*).

In the sections that follow, I walk you through how to conjugate *regular* (weak) and *irregular* (strong) verbs in the simple past.

Creating the simple past with regular (weak) verbs

Regular verbs are the ones that don't have a stem change between the present tense and the simple past tense. For example, the present tense stem of **wohnen** is **wohn-**, and the simple past stem is also **wohn-**. The endings are what make the difference between the two tenses.

Here's how to form the simple past of regular verbs:

1. Take the **-en** off the infinitive.

2. Add **-te,** which I refer to as the *-te tense marker.*

3. Add the additional endings (with the exception of the **ich** and **er/sie/es** forms, which have no ending other than **-te**). The endings are as follows: nothing, **-st,** nothing, **-n, -t, -n,** and **-n.**

Compare the present and the simple past of the verb **wohnen** (*to live*). The present form is in parentheses after the simple past.

wohnen (*to live*) — Simple Past (Present)	
ich wohn**te** (wohn**e**)	wir wohn**ten** (wohn**en**)
du wohn**test** (wohn**st**)	ihr wohn**tet** (wohn**t**)
er/sie/es wohn**te** (wohn**t**)	sie wir wohn**ten** (wohn**en**)
Sie wohn**ten** (wohn**en**)	
Ich **wohnte** in Dortmund. (*I lived in Dortmund.*)	

A second group of regular verbs are those with a stem ending in **-d** or **-t.** (Note that a few verbs with the stem ending in **-fn** or **-gn** also fall into this category.) With these verbs, you put an additional **e** in front of the **-te** tense marker. Taking **arbeiten** (*to work*) as an example, you form the simple past like this: **ich arbeit + e + -te = ich arbeitete.**

arbeiten (*to work*) — Simple Past (Present)	
ich arbeit**ete** (arbeite)	wir arbeit**eten** (arbeit**en**)
du arbeit**etest** (arbeit**est**)	ihr arbeit**etet** (arbeit**et**)
er/sie/es arbeit**ete** (arbeit**et**)	sie arbeit**eten** (arbeit**en**)
Sie arbeit**eten** (arbeit**en**)	
Du **arbeitetest** sehr schnell. (*You worked very fast.*)	

Creating the simple past with irregular (strong) verbs

The group of verbs in this section is called *irregular* because unlike regular verbs, these verbs have a variety of vowel changes in the simple past form. The changes may simply be one vowel change, such as **i** to **a**; with the irregular verb **beginnen** (*to begin*), the simple past stem is **begann** (*began*).

To conjugate irregular verbs in the simple past, note the following:

> ✔ These verbs have no endings in **ich** and **er/sie/es** forms.
>
> ✔ The other endings, those for **du, wir, ihr, sie,** and **Sie,** are the same as the present tense endings. The endings are nothing, **-st**, nothing, **-en, -t, -en,** and **-en.**

beginnen (*to begin*)	
ich begann	wir begann**en**
du begann**st**	ihr begann**t**
er/sie/es begann	sie begann**en**
Sie begann**en**	
Er **begann** zu laufen. (*He began to run.*)	

Luckily for you, German has a fairly small number of irregular verbs for you to worry about when conjugating the simple past tense. In addition, some of them resemble English irregular verbs in both spelling and meaning. Table 7-7 lists verbs that are irregular in both German and English.

Past participle: gedacht; Auxiliary verb: haben

Present subjunctive: würde denken

Present: denk**e**, denk**st**, denk**t**, denk**en**, denk**t**, denk**en**, denk**en**

Simple past: dach**te**, dach**test**, dach**te**, dach**ten**, dach**tet**, dach**ten**, dach**ten**

Imperative: denk/denk**e**, denk**t**, denk**en** Sie

Other verbs like this are listed in Table A-2.

Strong Verbs

Verbs with auxiliary haben

trinken (to drink)

Present tense stem: trink-

Simple past (1st/3rd-person singular): trank

Past participle: getrunken; Auxiliary verb: haben

Present subjunctive: würde trinken

Present: trink**e**, trink**st**, trink**t**, trink**en**, trink**t**, trink**en**, trink**en**

Simple past: trank, trank**st**, trank, trank**en**, trank**t**, tran**ken**, trank**en**

Imperative: trink/trink**e**, trink**t**, trink**en** Sie

Other verbs like this are listed in Table A-2.

Verbs with auxiliary sein

kommen (to come)

Present tense stem: komm-

Simple past (1st/3rd-person singular): kam

Past participle: gekommen; Auxiliary verb: sein

Present subjunctive: würde kommen

Present: komme, kommst, kommt, kommen, kommt, kommen, kommen

Simple past: kam, kamst, kam, kamen, kamt, kamen, kamen

Imperative: komm/komme, kommt, kommen Sie

Other verbs like this are listed in Table A-2.

Verbs with present-tense vowel change in 2nd- and 3rd-person singular

lesen (to read)

Present tense stem: les-; Present-tense vowel change: liest

Simple past (1st/3rd-person singular): las

Past participle: gelesen; Auxiliary verb: haben

Present subjunctive: würde lesen

Present: lese, **liest, liest,** lesen, lest, lesen, lesen

Simple past: las, lasest/last, las, lasen, last, lasen, lasen

Imperative: lies, lest, lesen Sie

Other verbs like this are listed in Table A-2.

Separable-Prefix Verbs

mitbringen (to bring along)

Present tense stem: bring- mit

Simple past (1st/3rd-person singular): brachte mit

Past participle: mitgebracht; Auxiliary verb: haben

Present subjunctive: würde mitbringen

Present: bringe mit, bringst mit, bringt mit, bringen mit, bringt mit, bringen mit, bringen mit

Simple past: brachte mit, brachtest mit, brachte mit, brachten mit, brachtet mit, brachten mit, brachten mit

Imperative: bring mit/bringe mit, bringt mit, bringen Sie mit

Some other similar verbs are **anhaben** (*to wear*), **anrufen** (*to telephone*), **fernsehen** (*to watch TV*), and **vorhaben** (*to plan*).

Inseparable-Prefix Verbs (Without Ge- Prefix in the Past Participle)

Verbs with a past participle ending in -t

bezahlen (to pay)

Present tense stem: bezahl-

Simple past (1st/3rd-person singular): bezahl**te**

Past participle: bezahl**t**; Auxiliary verb: haben

Present subjunctive: würde bezahlen

Present: bezahl**e**, bezahl**st**, bezahl**t**, bezahl**en**, bezahl**t**, bezahl**en**, bezahl**en**

Simple past: bezahl**te**, bezahl**test**, bezahl**te**, bezahl**ten**, bezahl**tet**, bezahl**ten**, bezahl**ten**

Imperative: bezahle, bezahlt, bezahlen Sie

Some other verbs like this are **beantworten** (*to answer*), **besuchen** (*to visit*), **erklären** (*to explain*), **gehören** (*to belong to*), and **versuchen** (*to try*).

Verbs with a past participle ending in -en

gefallen (to like)

Present tense stem: gefall-

Present-tense vowel change (in 2nd/3rd-person singular): gefäll-

Simple past (1st/3rd-person singular): gefiel

Past participle: gefallen; Auxiliary verb: haben

Present subjunctive: würde gefallen

Present: gefalle, gefällst, gefällt, gefallen, gefallt, gefallen, gefallen

Simple past: gefiel, gefielst, gefiel, gefielen, gefielt, gefielen, gefielen

Imperative: gefall/gefalle, gefallt, gefallen Sie

Other verbs like this are listed in Table A-2, at the end of the chapter.

Auxiliary Verbs Haben, Sein, and Werden

haben (to have)

Present (and auxiliary for verbs using haben in present perfect): habe, hast, hat, haben, habt, haben, haben

Simple past (1st/3rd-person singular): hatte

Past participle: gehabt; Auxiliary verb: haben

Present subjunctive (same as simple past with umlaut): hätte, hättest, hätte, hätten, hättet, hätten, hätten

Simple past: hatte, hattest, hatte, hatten, hattet, hatten, hatten

Imperative: hab/habe, habt, haben Sie

sein (to be)

Present (and auxiliary for verbs using sein in present perfect): bin, bist, ist, sind, seid, sind, sind

Simple past (1st/3rd-person singular): war

Past participle: gewesen; Auxiliary verb: sein

Present subjunctive: wäre, wärest, wäre, wären, wäret, wären, wären

Simple past: war, warst, war, waren, wart, waren, waren

Imperative: sei, seid, seien Sie

werden (to become, shall, will)

Present: werde, wirst, wird, werden, werdet, werden

Simple past (1st/3rd-person singular): wurde

Past participle: geworden; Auxiliary verb: sein

Present subjunctive (same as simple past with umlaut): würde, würdest, würde, würden, würdet, würden, würden

Simple past: wurde, wurdest, wurde, wurden, wurdet, wurden, wurden

Imperative: werde, werdet, werden Sie

Note that the present of **werden** is the auxiliary verb for forming the future tense, and the present subjunctive is the auxiliary verb for many verbs in the present subjunctive.

Modal Auxiliary Verbs Dürfen, Können, Mögen, Müssen, Sollen, and Wollen

dürfen (to be allowed, may)

Present: darf, darfst, darf, dürfen, dürft, dürfen, dürfen

Simple past (1st/3rd-person singular): durfte

Past participle: gedurft; Auxiliary verb: haben

Present subjunctive (same as simple past with umlaut): dürfte

Simple past: durfte, durftest, durfte, durften, durftet, durften, durften

können (to be able to, can, to know how to do something)

Present: kann, kannst, kann, können, könnt, können, können

Simple past (1st/3rd-person singular): konnte

Past participle: gekonnt; Auxiliary verb: haben

Present subjunctive (same as simple past with umlaut): **könnte**

Simple past: konn**te**, konn**test**, konn**te**, konn**ten**, konn**tet**, konn**ten**, konn**ten**

mögen (to like [to], want to)

Present: mag, mag**st**, mag, mög**en**, mög**t**, mög**en**, mög**en**

Simple past (1st/3rd-person singular): moch**te**

Past participle: gemocht; Auxiliary verb: haben

Present subjunctive (same as simple past with umlaut): **möch**te (*would like to*)

Simple past: moch**te**, moch**test**, moch**te**, moch**ten**, moch**tet**, moch**ten**, moch**te**

müssen (to have to, must)

Present: muss, muss**t**, muss, müss**en**, müss**t**, müss**en**, müss**en**

Simple past (1st/3rd-person singular): muss**te**

Past participle: gemusst; Auxiliary verb: haben

Present subjunctive (same as simple past with umlaut): **müss**te

Simple past: muss**te**, muss**test**, muss**te**, muss**ten**, muss**tet**, muss**ten**, muss**ten**

sollen (to be supposed to, should)

Present: soll, soll**st**, soll, soll**en**, soll**t**, soll**en**, soll**en**

Simple past (1st/3rd-person singular): soll**te**

Past participle: gesollt; Auxiliary verb: haben

Present subjunctive (same as simple past): soll**te**

Simple past: soll**te**, soll**test**, soll**te**, soll**ten**, soll**tet**, soll**ten**, soll**ten**

wollen (to want to)

Present: will, will**st**, will, woll**en**, woll**t**, woll**en**, woll**en**

Simple past (1st/3rd-person singular): woll**te**

Past participle: gewollt; Auxiliary verb: haben

Present subjunctive (same as simple past): woll**te**

Simple past: woll**te,** woll**test,** woll**te,** woll**ten,** woll**tet,**
woll**ten,** woll**ten**

Principal Parts of Verbs

Table A-2 contains high-frequency strong verbs, irregular
weak verbs, modal auxiliaries, common separable-prefix verbs
whose base verb isn't listed, **haben** (*to have*), and **sein** (*to be*).
The past participles that use the auxiliary **sein** are indicated;
the others use **haben.**

Table A-2   Principal Parts of Verbs

Infinitive	Stem Change (3rd-Person Singular Present)	Simple Past	Past Participle	English Meaning
anfangen	fängt an	fing an	angefangen	to start, begin
anrufen		rief an	angerufen	to telephone
beginnen		begann	begonnen	to begin
bekommen		bekam	bekommen	to get
bleiben		blieb	ist geblieben	to stay
brechen	bricht	brach	gebrochen	to break
bringen		brachte	gebracht	to bring
denken		dachte	gedacht	to think
dürfen	darf	durfte	gedurft	to be permitted to, may
einladen	lädt ein	lud ein	eingeladen	to invite
empfehlen	empfiehlt	empfahl	empfohlen	to recommend
entscheiden		entschied	entschieden	to decide
essen	isst	aß	gegessen	to eat
fahren	fährt	fuhr	ist gefahren	to go, drive, travel
fallen	fällt	fiel	ist gefallen	to fall
finden		fand	gefunden	to find

(continued)

Table A-2 *(continued)*

Infinitive	Stem Change (3rd-Person Singular Present)	Simple Past	Past Participle	English Meaning
fliegen		flog	ist geflogen	to fly
geben	gibt	gab	gegeben	to give
gefallen	gefällt	gefiel	gefallen	to like
gehen		ging	ist gegangen	to go
gewinnen		gewann	gewonnen	to win
haben	hat	hatte	gehabt	to have
halten	hält	hielt	gehalten	to hold, stop
heißen		hieß	geheißen	to be called, named
helfen	hilft	half	geholfen	to help
kennen		kannte	gekannt	to know (person)
kommen		kam	ist gekommen	to come
können	kann	konnte	gekonnt	to be able to, can
lassen	lässt	ließ	gelassen	to let
laufen	läuft	lief	ist gelaufen	to run
lesen	liest	las	gelesen	to read
liegen		lag	gelegen	to lie (situated)
mögen	mag	mochte	gemocht	to like
müssen	muss	musste	gemusst	to have to, must
nehmen	nimmt	nahm	genommen	to take
schlafen	schläft	schlief	geschlafen	to sleep
schließen		schloss	geschlossen	to close
schreiben		schrieb	geschrieben	to write
schwimmen		schwamm	ist geschwommen	to swim
sehen	sieht	sah	gesehen	to see
sein	ist	war	ist gewesen	to be

Infinitive	Stem Change (3rd-Person Singular Present)	Simple Past	Past Participle	English Meaning
singen		sang	gesungen	to sing
sitzen		saß	gesessen	to sit
sollen	soll	sollte	gesollt	to be supposed to, should
sprechen	spricht	sprach	gesprochen	to speak
stehen		stand	gestanden	to stand
sterben	stirbt	starb	ist gestorben	to die
tragen	trägt	trug	getragen	to wear, carry
treffen	trifft	traf	getroffen	to meet
trinken		trank	getrunken	to drink
tun		tat	getan	to do
vergessen	vergisst	vergaß	vergessen	to forget
verlieren		verlor	verloren	to lose
verstehen		verstand	verstanden	to understand
waschen	wäscht	wusch	gewaschen	to wash
werden	wird	wurde	ist geworden	to become, will
wissen	weiß	wusste	gewusst	to know (fact)
wollen	will	wollte	gewollt	to want (to)

Index